GLORY
ON YOUR
HOUSE

To Sue & Mike
May His glory
fill your "new
house" and over
flow into all areas.
Love in Christ,
Jayce & Mike
Marcha

GLORY
ON YOUR
HOUSE

JACK HAYFORD

✓ chosen books

FLEMING H. REVELL COMPANY
TARRYTOWN, NEW YORK

This greatly expanded and revised work contains much of the original *The Church on the Way* by Jack Hayford, published by Chosen Books, 1982.

The lyrics on pages 266–267 by Eli Chavira © 1971, 1980 *Scripture in Song,* administered by Maranatha! Music, are used with permission.

The paragraph on p. 276 from *A Severe Mercy,* © 1977, 1980 by Sheldon Vanauken, is used with permission of Harper Collins.

Unless noted otherwise, Scripture quotations in this publication are from The New King James Version. Copyright © 1979, 1980, 1982 Thomas Nelson, Inc., Publishers.

Scripture quotations identified NASB are from the New American Standard Bible, copyright © The Lockman Foundation 1960, 1962, 1963, 1968, 1971, 1972, 1973, 1975, 1977.

Scripture quotations identified KJV are from the King James Version of the Bible.

Library of Congress Cataloging-in-Publication Data

Hayford, Jack W.
  Glory on your house / Jack Hayford.
    p. cm.
  Sequel to: The church on the way / Jack W. Hayford.
  ISBN 0-8007-9190-8
  1. Christian life—1960– 2. Glory of God. 3. Presence of God.
I. Hayford, Jack W. Church on the way. II. Title.
BV4501.2.H36874 1991
248.4—dc20   91-24345
                                                    CIP

A Chosen book
Copyright © 1982, 1991 by Jack W. Hayford
Chosen Books Publishing Company, Ltd.
Published by
Fleming H. Revell Company
Tarrytown, New York
Printed in the United States of America

Acknowledging Glory-Giving Grace

God's grace is *endlessly* amazing.

The excellence of His ability to exceed anything and everything I could ask, think or do is a continual source of awe—and I praise Him:

—for the continuous delight of *abiding* grace, which has attended our "on the way" experience of over two decades, and sustained "glory"; and

—for an unexpected *surge* of grace that made the renewing and expanding of an earlier told story *truly* "glorious"; and

—for the patient grace of editors like Jane Campbell at Chosen, and servant-spirited secretaries like Lana Duim, Renee McCarter and Janet Kemp, whose help often causes me to shout, "Glory!"; and,

—for Rebecca Bauer—Anna's and my dear daughter *Becki*—whose dedication in labor and brilliance in accomplishment when we attempt such projects as this is a *grace-gift* of *fresh* glory to our "house."

J.W.H.

Contents

Inviting You to "Glory"...

... might seem pretentious.

I hope not. Because it is not only a sincere invitation, but a credible one as well.

When I sat down to pen this book I wasn't expecting "glory" as I wrote. I have written too often to expect it to be fun or easy.

But something started to happen. And as it was happening I knew God's goodness was intending something unusual for *you*. It is my prayer that what I sensed will be received on your end of this process.

In writing this book in two sections—the first addressing personal living, the second to attend to church-family life—I have sought to emphasize the practical.

Spirituality isn't mystical, even though glory moments such as I describe early on do happen. But God's voice, His leadings and the manifestations of His Spirit have never been given to breed a cult of mystics or a band of bizarre babblers.

So as you begin, let me invite you to glory, but I extend the invitation with a promise: This is going to be a *practical* trip.

And I trust that as it concludes and the final pages are finished, you not only will have *tasted* glory, but will be ready to *test* its possibilities in the everyday of your journey with God.

In His strong love bonds,

Jack Hayford

Van Nuys, California

Part I

Glory on Your Life

1

Surprised by Glory

It was "perfect southern California"—a clear, crisp, sunshiny January day, the kind of wintertime weather that attracts the nation every year to its Western doorstep. It was Saturday, the day after New Year's. The Rose Bowl game had been played the day before following another globally televised parade of flower-festooned floats.

But even though the days are mild and sunny, the nights are frosty. So it was that the thermostat was on my mind.

I had spent the afternoon at my church office finalizing my message for the next day's service. *I must remember to set the thermostat before I leave,* I prompted myself, *so the sanctuary will be comfortable for the congregation as they gather tomorrow.* The wall clock read 4:30. I folded my sermon notes into my Bible, pleased that I was already done—prepared for the next day and on my way home early, without Anna's having to call me for dinner. I turned off the desk light and, closing the office door, walked into the small sanctuary. (Church attendance on any given Sunday barely exceeded one hundred.) As I strolled down the aisle toward the altar area and turned to the left where the thermostat was located on the front wall, I had no inkling of the remarkable thing that was about to happen.

I squinted at the numbers on the thermostat dial, set it at 72 degrees, then turned to leave the room. At that instant I was stopped in my tracks. I stood by the piano, bewildered.

The room was filled with a silvery mist.

The late afternoon sun slanted through the stained-glass windows, adding to the beauty of the sight before me but in no way causing it. The mist had not been there a moment before. My mind probed for an answer: *This isn't dust . . . smog . . . is it?*

The real answer preceded the question, for my heart and my mind knew better. There was clearly no natural explanation for what I was seeing. No earthly dust had the glowing quality that this mist possessed as it filled the whole room, even where the sunlight was not shining.

I think I know what this is. My mind assessed the situation and drew a quick conclusion. *Glory.* But though I thought the thought, it was too grand, and I was fearful of admitting it even to myself.

Test it out first, my reason countered. *If this is something of God, it will stand up to scrutiny.*

I turned back toward the thermostat and stepped through the prayer room door beside it.

No mist there.

Then I rubbed my eyes before reentering the sanctuary. *If it's just me,* I mused, *that will take care of it.*

But now, standing within that humble little chapel again and scanning the scene before me, it was evident that something unusual and very real was there. The "mistiness" was still present.

As bewildering as the moment was, I was still neither startled nor frightened, for within my spirit I sensed this was surely something of God's doing. I also felt that I did, in fact, know what I was seeing. I was simply too reticent to claim as much to myself, for I had no reason to anticipate such a visitation.

Glory? The word was there again, but the question mark in my mind was added by the fact that I had never asked for, thought about or imagined such a thing as I was seeing.

Except that one time at the college.

It had been about a year earlier, just at the conclusion of a counseling session with one of the students. Having finished our talk, I had led us both in prayer—and as I lifted my eyes the same kind of mist had filled the room.

At first neither of us spoke. Then I ventured a slow gesture unfolding my hand outwardly, and inquired, "Do you—?"

Speechless, the student simply nodded, as both of us looked around the room from our seated positions. About fifteen seconds later the mist simply disappeared, as though it had been dialed away by a special effects technician's rheostat.

"And now it's gone," I observed, to see if the student's observations matched mine. My gaze met confirming eyes, and we looked at each other with puzzled consternation. We had each heard of the *shekinah*—the radiant, visible manifestation of God's glory that the Bible talks about. But seeing it—for we were both convinced that was what had happened—was something new for us both.

Now, on this winter day just inside a brand-new year,

I was witnessing it again. But two things were significantly different: No one was with me to confirm the vision, and I had not been at prayer, as on the other occasion. I felt a peculiar sense of wonder: Why this display? Also, strangely enough, I felt concerned that no one was there with whom I could confirm that I was not just seeing things.

I had not taken into consideration, however, that there *was* another witness. Whatever the reader may think of my next words, I know no way to tell it other than the way it occurred. The Lord spoke.

"It is what you think it is," the Voice said. It wasn't "spoken" as a sound in the room, but it was warm and comforting—unbegotten by my own thought processes yet crystal clear to my conscious "hearing."

The words were at once moving and peculiarly humorous. Imagine! The almighty God of the universe concerned with my worrying about a confirming witness and condescending to be that witness Himself. It was as though God were saying, "I see it too, Jack." That was almost engagingly, graciously funny.

But what most moved me, profoundly and deeply, were the words that followed:

"I have given My glory to dwell in this place."

I stood there silently. Awed. For the moment, dumbstruck. I had nothing to say and there seemed to be nothing to ask. I just waited. And moments later the scene returned to the ordinariness of mere sunlight filtered through stained-glass windows in the room.

Things were as they were before—and yet they weren't. I knew that glory was still there. There was no more Voice and no more mist, but glory nevertheless had come to this house.

*   *   *

Whenever I look back on that experience, it always seems strange that I did not feel inclined at the moment to do anything unusual. I remember thinking, *Thank You, Lord,* but otherwise I was relatively passive—overwhelmed and not knowing what one *could* do.

I did not fall prostrate in worship.

I did not stoop to remove my shoes, though it was certainly a "holy ground" setting.

I was possessed by no dominant emotion that I can describe.

It was in some ways so simple that I risk sounding irreverent to say so. I knew only that I had seen what I had seen and heard what I had heard. So I breathed another *Thank You, Lord* and went on home.

It is also peculiar that I didn't even think to tell Anna when I got home. (Every wife will rise to shout, "He's like *every* man! You can *never* get them to talk about what happened at work when they get home!") In fact, I told no one about the afternoon visitation for some time to come. But the implications of that day were to begin to be realized sooner than I could imagine.

In church the next day there were nearly 170 people!

That may be an unimpressive number to most people, but given the fact that a typical Sunday barely scratched beyond 100, it was astounding! Although it was the first Sunday of a new year, there was nothing of particular moment that had been scheduled, promoted or trumpeted. In fact, we hardly had that many people on the rolls.

I watched the doors as they continued to swing inward time after time as worshipers appeared. As we sang the opening hymn I had a difficult time concentrating on its theme. (*Wow! Look at this crowd!*) It must have brought a chuckle to the Almighty, who knew what was happening. He was beginning something I didn't even realize. For, strange as it may seem, I was not making any association between the assembling crowd and the incident of the day before in this very sanctuary.

The fact is, however, that from that day until this, an increasing number of people have walked through those doors, and the other doors that have replaced them as progressive building programs have provided expanding facilities for The Church On The Way. At the time of this writing, a typical week will find approximately 10,000 in the combined attendance of all services and meetings convened here.

But reporting the growth of one congregation is not the purpose of my writing. Rather, I want to relate some of the lessons about glory that have unfolded to us during the years since that marvelous moment. I am anxious to do so because of a deep-seated conviction I hold, one I believe is rooted in God's Word and grounded in His grace. I am convinced that God is ready to visit *your* house with His glory, persuaded that it is intended to be the joyous realization of anyone. I believe glory is God's promise of His radiant presence—whether seen or unseen—available to any individual, family or group who will align with His divine order.

Years passed following that memorable Saturday before I shared publicly the story of that afternoon, because I realized it could be sorely misunderstood. But from that day to this—without any notable plan, other than seeking to be faithful to those biblical principles the Holy Spirit has made alive in our hearts—The Church On The Way has grown. Still, we know it is His gift of glory that has been the key to this joyful realization of God's blessing and fruitfulness.

Three Lessons About Glory

Certain points of understanding about glory have imprinted themselves upon us as time has passed. Because it is likely that you desire God's visitation of His glory-filled blessing upon your heart, home or enterprise, look with me at some of the concepts we discovered.

First, God does desire to manifest His glory among His people.

> Arise, shine; for your light has come! And the glory of the Lord is risen upon you. For behold, the darkness shall cover the earth, and deep darkness the people; but the Lord will arise over you, and His glory will be seen upon you. Isaiah 60:1–2

This was new to me! From my earliest memory, I had always thought God jealous about His glory, as though protectively (if not grandiosely) unwilling to allow anyone else to share in it. It was only when He addressed my experience with the word "I have given My glory to dwell in this place" that I searched the Scriptures.

Throughout my years of upbringing in church I had heard the oft-quoted words "My glory will I not give to another." They were formidable words to my mind, issuing more than a warning—words conveying something of a divine decree intended to "put man in his place." If that's what God's Word said—and if my experience contradicted it—I was ready to renounce my experience in absolute, ready deference to the eternal Word engraved in the Scriptures.

My study, however, opened my understanding of God's great-heartedness regarding His glory. Indeed, Isaiah's prophecy did and does emphasize God's refusal to share His glory with another. But the text clearly defines exactly who "another" is:

> "I am the Lord, that is My name; and My glory I will not give to another, nor My praise to graven images."   Isaiah 42:8

It was sheer revelation to me. God's edict against sharing *any* of His glory is clear—but it is confined to His enemies. He wills that nothing of His excellency, majesty or glory be compromised or companioned in by other gods—demon deities who boast themselves against Him.

In distinct contrast, listen to Jesus' disclosure of the Father's heart. Concerning the Church, His own redeemed ones who honor God's Messiah and who have received His witness, the Savior prays that

> " . . . the glory which You [Father] gave Me I have given them [all who receive Jesus], that they may be one just as We are one. . . ."   John 17:22

Christ Himself, who embodies the fullness of God's glory, has clearly expressed His will and desire that God's glory be transmitted to and enjoyed by His Church, "which is His body, the fullness of Him who fills all in all" (Ephesians 1:23).

That lesson opened the door for me to *expect* glory—to

believe God is as happy for your house to know it as He is mine.

Second, we learned that God's glory is associated with worship, and that those who fill the house with praise pave the way for glory. The Scriptures plainly show, for example, that God's visible glory was manifested when His priorities and patterns of worship were honored by His people. We can see this at the time the Tabernacle of Moses was completed.

> And he raised up the court all around the tabernacle and the altar, and hung up the screen of the court gate. So Moses finished the work. Then the cloud covered the tabernacle of meeting, and the glory of the Lord filled the tabernacle. And Moses was not able to enter the tabernacle of meeting, because the cloud rested above it, and the glory of the Lord filled the tabernacle.   Exodus 40:33–35

The same thing happened in Solomon's time. At the dedication of his Temple, when the priests had led in a lavish display of worship according to the Scriptures, the record shows that

> it came to pass, when the trumpeters and singers were as one, to make one sound to be heard in praising and thanking the Lord, and when they lifted up their voice with the trumpets and cymbals and instruments of music, and praised the Lord, saying: "For He is good, for His mercy endures forever," that the house, the house of the Lord, was filled with a cloud, so that the priests could not continue ministering because of the cloud; for the glory of the Lord filled the house of God.   2 Chronicles 5:13–14

Full-hearted, biblically ordered, Holy Spirit–ignited worship introduces the glorious order of the Eternal One. "I will glorify the house of My glory," the Lord declares, adding, "I will make the place of My feet glorious" (Isaiah 60:7, 13).

In short, where people worship God humbly, forthrightly and obediently, according to His Word, He will respond with a distinct show of His presence. Worship-filled praise invites the rule of His glorious Kingdom and He enters with loving blessings and liberating power. Honoring God's Word in our lives, exalting God's Son with our lips and giving the Holy Spirit a place to work by the love we show God and man allow distinct and marvelous blessing to pour forth.

None of this is the heritage of a limited group or select breed or certain denomination, or even of those of a particular doctrinal stripe. And it is not the portion of a charismatic Christian as opposed to a noncharismatic, nor of a Protestant believer as opposed to a Catholic. Neither is it only for "at church." Homes, families, people and places may welcome God's glory. As the Bible teaches it, His glory may become the increasing portion of anyone who pursues a pathway of humility before His throne. God is looking for people like that—to whom to show the glory of His excellence and the excellence of His glory.

This does not mean you have to have a vision of something visible, as I did. God may be noticeably present in glory and power without any such manifestation. The Hebrew word translated "glory" helps us grasp this, in that it is also the word for "weight." When the Bible speaks of "the glory" it is not speaking so much of something aglow as of something with substantial force to it. Glory isn't something flimsy, ethereal, intangible.

Rather, when the glory of God is in a place, something forceful, weighty, mighty is present in the spiritual realm. People can recognize it. They will want to be there. Mankind longs intuitively for the fulfillment and restoration, the focus and fruitfulness, that attend the soul reintroduced to lost glory.

Created to know the presence of God's glory, men and women yearn for its reality while little understanding the path to its recovery. Mankind needs not only forgiveness for sin but the fulfillment that sin deprives him of. As Adam and Eve snatched for leaves to cover themselves, so humankind still attempts desperately not only to cover up the fact of our naked sinfulness before God, but to substitute something for the loss of being clothed in glory. The splendor of God's presence was essentially what man wore before the Fall. Thus, the first couple's sudden awareness had less to do with their nudity than with their sense of glory that had departed.

Absent glory characterizes fallen man, whether the first ones stripped of glory by sin's entry, or in our own case as members of a race who "fall short of the glory of God" (Romans 3:23). We know instinctively we need "the weight of glory" added to our lives; thus we pursue reputation, acceptance, possessions, education—something in which we might glory. The real quest is for substance—*weight;* and such alternate pursuits, not evil in themselves, are not to be condemned. But neither can they be commended apart from finding the fountainhead of glory in Christ *first!* "Christ in you, the hope of glory" (Colossians 1:27); and anything or anyone less never satisfies. Substitutes become gods that hold no weight and provide no abiding glory. The only goal that will fully grant the desire for "weight," for substance to our lives, is to become clothed again in the glory of God.

Third, we learned that God's glory must be entertained—that is, honored so as not to be lost. To "entertain" God's glory is to welcome His workings in our hearts and homes, our churches and congregations, just as we would a beloved guest. My own church has learned the danger of becoming "accustomed" to His grace. Glory is the portion of those who glorify Him, and true worship springs only from hearts that are being constantly renewed in a childlike first love.

Neglect, sophistication, even well-intended but dulling habit, will diminish glory to whatever degree the will of the flesh or the pride of the human heart persists in its own way. Samson is a disturbing photograph of this possibility.

Following his carnal indulgence and surrender to Delilah's connivings, we find him shorn of his hair. The glory he offered God through obedience was gone, and the glory his obedience had invited upon his life, resulting in excelling strength and ability, was gone with it. It's a sad episode.

> And [Delilah] said, "The Philistines are upon you, Samson!" So he awoke from his sleep, and said, "I will go out as before, at other times, and shake myself free!" *But he did not know that the Lord had departed from him.*
>
> Judges 16:20 (author's emphasis)

God's gift of unique blessing upon Samson was "entertained" by his continuing in his vow to walk in God's ways. The tragedy is double, not only that he lost God's presence, but worse—that he didn't even recognize it was gone until he was crippled at the hands of his enemy!

Over the years the Holy Spirit has reproved me and our congregation. Any style of worship can become habitual, ritualized and tinny instead of fresh, wholehearted and vibrant. It is an incredible fact: Our hearts can become as hardened *to* the presence of God as they can *against* it. A church can be deceived, thinking its growth verifies the congregation's righteousness. An individual, similarly, can be deluded by the notion that his or her prosperity is God's seal of approval. A magnificent home may seem to attest to glorious achievement.

This is all a delusion. Well-managed churches, businesses, careers and dwellings can be built with or without God. But without God the day inevitably comes when, like Samson, we say, "I will go out as before, at other times, and shake myself free," and nothing happens. And in these words we hear the echo of thousands who have "learned all the moves" to achieve apparent success, but who have discovered that glory does not reside in our systems or structures, but in our simplicity of dependence on God.

God's glory was revealed that day—an unforgettable moment. And just as I have seen its fruit at this house, I long to see it at yours, too.

There *is* a way to bring His glory to your home address!

2

Glory on Your House

Prophets are a curious kind of people; they "see" things. *Seer* is that sticky word applied today to any crystal-gazing guru or prognosticator of events, however crazy and regardless of how seldom he or she is right. But *seer* used to be reserved for people who truly knew God. Real Bible prophets gave their forecasts in two ways—preaching and predicting. They would tell the people, "This is how *you* look in the eyes of heaven, and this is how *things* will come to look if nothing changes." In short, their message was, "If things don't get better *with* you, they're gonna get real bad *for* you. Signed, God."

Prophets were seldom popular people.

More often than not the lives of those they were addressing were so crammed with self-centered living and overflowing with corrupt, crude and corrosive behavior that their message was of necessity a stinging rebuke from heaven. The bleakness of quality in the lifestyle being confronted usually guaranteed that the house of cards built by such living was about to collapse. And the prophet would say so: "Look, your house is left to you desolate!" Such promises of future ruin hardly made a hit. But then, prophets never seemed interested in winning popularity contests anyway.

Isaiah was such a prophet.

In the middle of a muddled time in his city and nation, Isaiah spoke forth "the word of the Lord." As a seer, his proclamation against sin and of impending judgment led his hearers on a tour of sights less than desirably scenic. His hometown, urban Jerusalem, was filled with "filth" (that was his word for it!). He described a society shot through with moral perversion, relational and religious hypocrisy, confused families where parents had lost control of their kids, and a bevy of other problems resulting from a corrupted core of living. The city was coming unglued as hunger, drought, violence, homelessness and pornography (the idolatry of Isaiah's time) ransacked the community. Further, men were being emasculated by the impact of a feminist revival—a dynamic that was stripping the culture of almost anyone who had any understanding of true self-worth and of how a truly fulfilling life could possibly be lived.

Sound familiar?

It was a tough environment for housekeeping, not a lot different than the setting of our cities and towns today, where people like you and me are trying to cultivate roots, raise a family, develop a career and live a life of vibrant faith. And if Isaiah's first forecast for Jerusalem's demise told the whole story, it would appear that the prospects are as bleak for a "glory house" in our time as they were circa 750 B.C.

But Isaiah had a second word, a brighter hope: "In that day the Branch of the Lord shall be beautiful and glorious," he began (4:2). Like the saintly seers of old, he envisioned a day in which God would rebuild society by redeeming people and their homes. He opened with a figure that describes the Savior, the bringer of the future's promise.

"The Branch of the Lord" is a classic image prophets used to describe Messiah—Jesus Himself. Isaiah relates Messiah's rise "as a root out of dry ground" to show His inauguration into a human scene with seemingly little hope for great success (53:1–2). Other prophets advanced the vision: "Messiah shall be cut off," Daniel declares (9:26), pointing to apparent death and defeat. But Jeremiah 33:15 forecasts His recovery and anticipates the fruit of His work: "In those [future] days . . . I will cause to grow up to David [Messiah's line] a Branch of righteousness [i.e., renewed growth that brings about just and joyous living]."

The prophecies converge by describing God doing a work that is both "beautiful" (the Hebrew word relates to something conspicuously and prominently splendid and pleasant) and "glorious"—filled with His glory! It is all packed with promise, but the most remarkable thing centers in one outstanding fact: *All this will take place right at home—in the houses where people live!*

Let's grasp the full significance of this:

1. We are being shown something about people who live in "last times," whose lives are surrounded by the same kind of creeping corruption that has always beset our fallen race.

2. These people will find in Messiah's *rise* (His life), *ruin* (His death) and *recovery* (His resurrection) a blossoming brightness for their lives.

3.   The epicenter of this shakeup that turns on the lights in darkened lives is going to be at home! It is the promise of glory on your house. Listen to it:

> When the Lord has washed away the filth [by the Holy Spirit through Messiah's workings] ... then the Lord will create above every dwelling place of Mount Zion, and above her assemblies, a cloud and smoke by day and the shining of a flaming fire by night. For *over all the glory there will be a covering.*
> Isaiah 4:4–5 (author's emphasis)

The meaning of this terminology may elude someone who doesn't know the background of the prophet's words. But to everybody he addressed, the message was clear: "God is going to fill your house with His glory the same way He did Moses' Tabernacle and Solomon's Temple!" To Isaiah's hearers, this meant far more than a religious experience in a religious place. It promised that the presence of God would bring hope, healing, wholeness and happiness *right where I live!*

The cloud was no spooky mistiness but a radiant presence. The smoke and fire were not some contrived display on the order of "the wonderful Wizard of Oz." Rather, the protective covering of the almighty God was forecast to ensure both the *warm* flame of His presence to bless His people and the *warring* firepower of His wrath to battle against their enemies. The prophet was foretelling the possibility of homes like yours and mine being lighted with the glow of God's love, filled with the brightness of His blessing and defended by the fire of His fury on any attempts of the adversary.

I never understood this truth until He visited the

"house" of our church with glory. It was a case of both private and public blessing: private, in that it was my personal experience; and public, in that it affected my work and the people I touched. Both features of our lives are included and should not be overlooked. The glory Isaiah prophesied was promised to Zion's dwelling places and assemblies and the implications are multiple.

In this usage, *Zion* is that classic term often used to describe the people of God. Derived from the name of a topographical rise that constitutes part of the physical terrain of the city of Jerusalem, *Mount Zion* is used to name that hill (1 Kings 8:1; Psalm 48:2); to refer to God's redeemed sons and daughters (Psalm 147:12; Isaiah 52:1–2); and to describe the ultimate place of our gathering in worship—the heavenly Jerusalem (Hebrews 12:22; Revelation 14:1). By every description, Isaiah's prophecy makes clear God's intention to bring the bright benedictions of heavenly glory right into our everyday world. This intent deserves to be perceived in all its practical potential so we will see the full target in God's plan.

Remember the instance I recounted of God's glorious visitation on that Saturday afternoon? I said then that my point was not so much to relay the marvel of the moment as to give an explanation for the incredible overflow of blessing that has followed at our "house"—a congregation called The Church On The Way. So again, keeping our focus requires a reassertion: Glory is not something mystical but something mighty, something practical and powerful. And when God speaks about times like ours, declaring His will and desire to visit every house with glory, it is good for us to do more than cultivate a quest for a visible manifestation. My objective is not to urge you to look for a glow in earthly buildings.

It is to urge you to expect God's glory—the excellence of His blessings and works—in your daily circumstances and personal environment.

A study of the biblical idea of *house* may help us gain perspective on the broad dimensions the Lord wants us to envisage when He promises glory on your house.

The Dimensions of Your "House"

Oikos is the word for "house" used throughout the New Testament. Its Hebrew counterpart, *bayith* (pronounced bah-yeeth), is derived from the verb *bawnaw,* the word generally meaning "to build." Both refer to a good deal more than the physical structure in which a person lives. The biblical concept of "house" includes at least four things: *real estate, relationships, responsibilities* and *realm of influence.*

1. My "house" as *real estate.*

By real estate I refer, of course, to the physical dwelling place of a person or group. It may be a mobile home, a condominium, a shack in Bangladesh, a mansion in Beverly Hills, a suburban tract home in Silicon Valley, an apartment in New York City or a flat in London. Further, it may be a storefront church on Chicago's South Side, a wood-frame Grange hall where some Kansas farmers worship, a cathedral in Paris, a balconied sanctuary in Buenos Aires, a house church hall in Scotland or a white clapboard colonial church in New England complete with bell tower, stained-glass windows, hand-tooled pews and historic burial vaults. All these are included in the terms *dwelling* and *assembly.* God wants us to make no mistake. He likes places where people welcome Him into their physical dwellings: "Let them make Me a sanctuary, that I may dwell among them. . . . And there I will meet with you" (Exodus 25:8, 22a).

2. My "house" as *relationships*.

The term *house* has ever been used to describe the immediate circle of one's family or intimate relationships. Poe's classic "Fall of the House of Usher" chronicles more than the collapse of the dwelling; it describes the deterioration of a family—virtually demon-infested unto the destruction of a clan. The spiritual insight and spine-tingling horror of that story—sad in the way it betrays something of Poe's own tormented soul—provides a practical insight.

Families and relationships involve far more than biological genetics; there are *spiritual* genetics, too. God's promise of "glory on your house" is intended to be understood as a promise with real and practical possibilities— that spiritual life power may be transmitted through your family as surely as hair color. He simply calls us to believe: "You will be saved, you and your household" (Acts 16:31).

He also wants to pour out His Spirit on our sons and daughters (Joel 2:28) and bless those relationships that come within the circle of our home or family life (Exodus 12:4). *Neighbors,* the Bible calls them, but these are clearly more than the people next door. We are talking about God's interest in glorifying with His presence all our intimate relationships and acquaintances.

3. My "house" as *responsibilities*.

This refers primarily to the duties of our work, career or daily business enterprises. "Moses . . . was faithful in all His house," the writer of the book of Hebrews reports (3:2), referring to Moses' fulfillment of his leadership duties and the completion of his God-appointed tasks. Still, it is to the physical house Moses built—the Tabernacle—that we usually attach the most significance when we remember "the glory."

But when we turn to that event in God's Word and look at the entire passage, we find the secret to that marvelous visitation of God's glory unveiled. Seven times we read, "As the Lord had commanded Moses" (Exodus 40:16, 19, 21, 25, 27, 29, 32). In other words, Moses' steadfast fidelity to observe the glory of God's authority through obedience resulted in the completion of "His house" with this realization: "So Moses finished the work. Then the cloud covered the tabernacle . . . and the glory of the Lord filled the tabernacle" (40:33–34).

The lesson is clear: The glory comes first into our lives and practical duties to prosper and fulfill our goals. Then, marvelous manifestations of far more than we ever imagined may occur—but when they do it is certain that very practical things occurred well beforehand. Any glory of an ethereal nature will be *preceded* by the glory of practical obedience and its consequent blessing.

Let's agree, then, holding to this understanding: If I never see a cloudy mist of glory, God's wonderful promise is still ready to fill my private home and personal workplace with His presence and blessing!

4. My "house" as *realm of influence.*

All of us have a scope of contact far broader than our closer relationships or our regular business associates. Years ago a research organization sought to assess the aegis of influence of individual people in different walks of life. The most striking discovery they made was not the enormity of the influence of highly visible persons. Rather, they were amazed at the surprising number of people influenced significantly by "the members of the community deemed 'unimportant.' "

Suddenly the term *unimportant* had disappeared. They found that in the course of one year even a virtually home-bound, reclusive and withdrawing individual made contact with more than fifty people. Many of these individuals were said to have left an impression on others sufficient to be gauged as "impacting."

Small wonder, then, that God wants to fill all our "house" with glory. Our most ordinary of circumstances often turn out to be so vastly more important than we think that we cannot afford to have them limited by anything less than God's light, warmth and blessing!

The Creation of a Covering

Isaiah's "glory on your house" prophecy describes both the *means* and the *meaning* of that blessing. We will examine all the richness of meaning in our next chapter. But first, let's look at the mighty *means* God commits to the begetting of "glory on your house." It's nothing less than the *creative power of God!* "The Lord will *create* above every dwelling place . . . the glory" (Isaiah 4:5).

Every Bible reader understands the verb *create*. It is in the first verse of the Book: "In the beginning God *created*. . . ." The promise in Isaiah of the creation of glory is precisely the same term, and filled with hope as the promise is breathed to us from God's heart by His Holy Spirit, as though He were saying:

"My child, do you wonder *how* My glory could ever visit your house? Does your heart wither before such a prospect? Do your circumstances and limitations, your failures or your weaknesses cause you to doubt such grand possibilities?

"Listen as your Lord would say to you:

"If I was able to save your soul from eternal darkness and put My Spirit within you, resurrecting your soul from the dead and bringing you into My Son's Kingdom of light, am I not able to recreate your circumstances?

"The Lord who has given you the new world of life and eternal hope through salvation is also able to create a new world where you live. He is the God of both—all *grace* and all *glory!* The grace by which He recreated you and gave you new life is able to create glory to give you new light, bringing new blessing to your home!"

Such "words" are not self-inspired, excitable ideas. They are at the heart of the truth that *the Creator is our God.* As God commissioned Isaiah to say elsewhere,

"I have made you hear new things from this time,
even hidden things, and you did not know them.
They are created now and not from the beginning;
and before this day you have not heard them."
Isaiah 48:6–7

Long ago the psalmist wrote, "Unless the Lord builds the house, they labor in vain who build it" (127:1). He reminded us of the futility of any expectation for a house of glory unless God's hand and power beget it. Thus, we are wise to let hope rise in proportion to His promise.

You may see only the dismal need of your marriage, the darkened condition of your home, the wearying situation at work, the lackluster nature of your influence for Christ.

Or you already have sparks of beginning in a romance, and you want more than the fires of passion; you want the pure flame of holy love.

Or you have already begun to see bright beginnings in your home life, but you want your family to experience abiding warmth, like that symbolized by the glow of a fireplace surrounded by loved ones on a winter evening.

Or you have seen the ignition of new effectiveness in your work, but you want God to bring this beyond a flashy beginning and establish it by the glory of His blessing on your enterprise.

Or. . . . Why don't you cite your own circumstance?

What is the darkest situation you face? What is the brightest possibility you hold? In either case or in both, describe them to Him and let these become the beginning place for God to show you the pathway to realizing "glory on your house."

The Pathway of Praise

The day the phenomenon of God's visitation captured my attention so dramatically, there was one thing I *did* grasp. While I did not yet understand how much God desires to give His glory, and I surely did not understand why He would deign to display it before my eyes in the way He chose, I did understand this: The glory was a response to our commitment to be a people of praise.

It had been more than two years since I had been introduced to concepts of praise that had not been taught to me before. It wasn't so much the way praise was practiced as it was the way praise was perceived. Although I had been reared on the words "The Lord inhabits the praises of His people," I didn't really know the meaning of those words.

To be precise, Psalm 22:3 in the King James Version reads, "But thou art holy, O thou that inhabitest the praises of Israel." Not only had the verse been misquoted, but the awesome content of the promise it held had been undisclosed to me.

Some contemporary translations render the verb *inhabit* as *enthroned*—an absolute improvement. The Hebrew *yawshawb* means at its most simple "to sit down." But the best translation of this verb depends, curiously, on the nature of the situation. It is used of a judge taking the bench, of a military band lying quietly in ambush, of a family settling into their house, of a couple joining in marriage. Since each verb "sits" in a distinct way, other terms may justifiably be used in translation to describe more exactly each sitting. The Lord is cast in this psalm coming as the King of the heavens—and *His* proper "sitting" is enthronement.

It may seem presumptuous to say that human beings can do anything to "seat" God on His throne, since the sovereign Creator of the universe needs neither our assistance nor our approval to be enthroned. But there is a subtle truth often overlooked by those who would assert God's sovereignty so quickly that they forget our own. The biblical fact is, God has given each of us a sovereign will, too. Absolute control of our personal destiny has been placed within our own decision-making power. Thus, in any matters that concern us—including all facets of our "house"—we are in full dominion. (That fact is often at the root of our problems!)

But here is God's powerful solution. The pathway of praise is the approach to life that opens the way for God to begin to move in, to fill our house with His glory. Thus, we have a *need* to praise, and there is a *way* to do it.

The need is so basic that Jesus included it in His prayer teaching called the Lord's Prayer. In His pattern for our prayers asking for such things as daily forgiveness, daily provision and daily power to overcome, He said we should pray, "Thy Kingdom come, Thy will be done on earth as it is in heaven." Those words should not be mistaken as projecting a dreamy idea about futuristic millennial conditions. The tense is *now!* Just as with the rest of the prayer, Jesus points toward the pathway of worship-filled praise when He says (and I paraphrase freely):

1. *Our Father in heaven* (and I thank You for that relationship You have given me through Your Son, my Savior),

2. *Hallowed be Your name* (for You are holy, and I worship You and revel in the beauty of Your completeness and excellence).

3. *Your Kingdom come* (for there is no rule of my wisdom or of human working that can bring about Your peace, power and blessing);

4. *Your will be done* (because I bow in full submission to declare, as did Your Son, "Not My will but Yours be done"),

5. *On earth as it is in heaven* (for there is no question Your will is exercised where Your throne is established).

So, dear God, I now invite with my praise Your enthronement in my "house"—in the matters of my life, my dwelling, my relationships, my business and my influence. I exercise my sovereign right to self-rule and surrender it to You. Come rule here ... and now.

There is, then, a fountainhead concept that opens the floodgates of God's glory into human circumstances: prayerful, praiseful, worshipful openness to His rule and His way. The benefits are incredible! As some people I'm about to introduce you to were amazed to discover.

3

Bringing the Glory Home

If praise is the *means* by which glory visits a house, what will be the *meaning* or the outflow of God's visitation?

David seemed to know—David of Bethlehem, the personality source of great stories and glorious songs.

Here is a man who had a way with warfare that could bring victory and a way with women that brought horrible defeat. The tales of his life are not simply ancient myths surviving the centuries because children love to hear them retold. They are incidents captured forever in the inspired pages of the Book the Holy Spirit has given us to point the way to salvation and to teach us wisdom for a fulfilling daily life.

David was more than the kid who killed a giant. He was a real person who endured incredible difficulty and rose beyond impossible odds, raised by God almighty Himself to become king of His people Israel. David was a man who understood God's heart; thus, his genius was not just "a penchant for spiritual things," and certainly not a result of one man's learning to manipulate the Almighty.

No one does that.

The living God is not a dimestore deity rubbing elbows with the likes of those mythological demigods of Mount Olympus. He is the Lord of heaven and the Creator of earth. And it was not only David's reverence for the awesome majesty of the Almighty that produced his understanding of the Lord, but also his insight into God's desire for intimacy. He knew God wanted to dwell with His people—up close, in every heart, with every family, in every home. This knowledge is what prompted David to prepare for a second Tabernacle—one separate from the one Moses had built!

Two Tabernacles in Israel

Because the Bible's record of the movement and location of the Tabernacle of Moses seems unspecific after Israel invaded Canaan, many have failed to note a remarkable fact. At one time, under David's leadership, a second Tabernacle was erected.

Though its establishment took place earlier, the most pointed reference to it follows David's death. After a full life and a dynamic and successful reign at God's direction, David's son Solomon is crowned as king.

> Now Solomon the son of David was strengthened in his kingdom, and the Lord his God was with him and exalted him exceedingly. . . . Then [he] . . . went to the high place that was at Gibeon; for the tabernacle of meeting with God was there, which Moses the servant of the Lord had made in the wilderness.

But David had brought up the ark of God from Kirjath Jearim to the place David had prepared for it, for he had pitched a tent for it at Jerusalem.

2 Chronicles 1:1, 3–4

This narrative is of importance for more than simple reasons of historical interest. It holds remarkable significance for two pertinent points of understanding: its prophetic portent and the method of its establishment.

Something about David's erecting this second worship center touched God's heart and unveiled the heart of His intent. The way the Bible speaks of David's Tabernacle discloses something of God's desire to draw close to His people. The prophetic Scriptures propound both the memory of this tent and its future.

The prophet Amos, while denouncing Israel's sin during a dark era of her history, declared God's word about the hope of a future day:

"On that day I will raise up the tabernacle of David, which has fallen down, and repair its damages; I will raise up its ruins, and rebuild it as in the days of old."

Amos 9:11

Why would God set Himself to recover a second Tabernacle, especially in a time when there wasn't even one (for by Amos' time Solomon's Temple had been built and Moses' Tabernacle dismantled)? The apparent reason focuses in the uniqueness of David's tent of worship as compared with Moses'.

Primarily, in David's tabernacle, the Ark of the Covenant was far more approachable. We find this in a story that unfolds with a rich mixture of triumph and tragedy in 2 Samuel 6. David brings the Ark to Jerusalem, placing that small, gold-covered, coffin-like box containing the tablets engraved with the Ten Commandments "in the midst of the tabernacle that David had erected for it" (2 Samuel 6:17). The event was attended with great joy and festive celebration, and God was obviously pleased, even though the complex structures of Moses' Tabernacle were not in place.

What was different? Most notably, the Ark was not hidden from view! Within the tent, which reverent worshipers could enter, the Ark, formerly behind sets of curtains, could plainly be seen.

In the chapter that follows, God visits David. An overwhelmingly beautiful set of promises is given as the prophet Nathan delivers God's word to David. It can all be summarized in the simple phrase "The Lord tells you that He will make you a house" (2 Samuel 7:11). The accompanying speech outlines a combination of promises that include blessing for a lifetime, the promise of eternal life and the establishing of a family line that will fulfill God's will in future years.

What more could anyone want for his or her "house"?

In response to this message, "King David went in and sat before the Lord" (verse 18). In that telling phrase the Scriptures indicate what, to that time, was unthinkable:

A man who was not high priest had entered the presence of the God of Israel, before the Ark, and was communing with God in personal intimacy!

The whole of the text makes clear that there was nothing glib or reckless about this change in tradition. But the rest of the Bible indicates that this was the earliest grasp anyone gained of what God's long-range target really was. He was more than hinting that His ultimate plan was to deal with mankind's sin in a way that would allow all people everywhere to know His presence—His blessing and His power—up close!

Tenderly.

Purifyingly.

Personally.

And right at home.

This intent of God's is so etched into the understanding of the Old Testament prophetic scheme that the prophet Amos' words (that God "will raise up the tabernacle of David") become pivotal for releasing human understanding in the New Testament. Just as the Old Covenant could not fulfill God's longing and mankind was distanced from God outside the Tabernacle, so in Acts the New Covenant sought to find practical entry. But a blockage occurred, another "distancing" to be dealt with.

As the number of Gentile converts began to swell, believers in Jerusalem, primarily Jewish followers of Jesus, were troubled by growing dissent over what should be expected of Gentile converts. "Yes, they may receive our Messiah," the Jewish sector seemed to conclude, "but they can't truly be God's people unless they observe our historic rite of circumcision."

The resolution of the problem, which came through a grand council convened to make a decision on this issue (Acts 15), was distilled from Amos' words quoted above. When the apostle James, chairman of the gathering, rose to quote that prophecy, it stirred a rich understanding in the council. The truth became secured with simple beauty, as though unfolding around a three-point proposition:

1. God taught David how to overcome barriers to human intimacy with God, and the Tabernacle David built is the symbol of that lesson.

2. Amos said that at the end of time, God would raise up that fallen Tabernacle, that the people of all the earth might know an intimate walk with Him.

3. Thus, in the first-century Church, the rite of circumcision needed to be rescinded as a requirement for fellowship with God. Circumcision had ceased to be an aid to faith and had become another obstacle to approaching God.

Just as David discovered that God wanted to come to *his* city, to *his* house, we may be sure God's desire is to come to *our* house—personally and intimately. But for this coming to take place, another key lesson waits to be gained from David's experience: How do we bring home the glory?

We have already seen from David's writings that praiseful worship is the pathway that welcomes God's presence. Let us now deepen our understanding as we examine David's experience. He might describe it this way: "An unfunny thing happened to me on the way to Jerusalem!"

Establishing the House with Praise

Years before, just prior to King Saul's reign and through carnal presumption and human folly, Israel had lost the Ark. That priceless, gold-covered box that contained the tablets of the Ten Commandments not only symbolized the presence of God; it was where He chose to meet His people. Historically the glory cloud had hovered about it, which seemed to suggest that God was "in the box." More superstition than faith presided in Israel at this time, and many people thought having the Ark would be a shortcut to success. It became a tragic misunderstanding. People who wanted God's power (but not really Him *personally*) thought foolishly that "fetching the Ark in crisis" could fix their problems. So as they faced impending defeat at the hands of their enemies, the people sent for the Ark, presuming it would be their lucky rabbit's foot and bring victory in battle (1 Samuel 4).

It didn't work. Even though they carried the Ark onto the battlefield, Israel's troops were decimated by the Philistine garrisons. The Ark of God fell into heathen hands, taken as the spoils of war and supposed evidence that Philistia's fish-god Dagon was superior to Yahweh, God of Israel. But a miraculous turn of events at the Ashdod temple of Dagon and a reversal of fortune among the Philistines made it clear to them: "If you don't know Yahweh, this Box is too hot to handle!" So the heathen troops built a cart, put the Ark on it, slapped the rumps of the oxen team drawing the cart and hoped to get the thing out of town (1 Samuel 5–6).

Even more amazing than how the Ark was returned to Israeli borders is Saul's indifference to it once he came to the throne. For years the Ark was left at a house in a town west of Jerusalem, rather than being returned to the Tabernacle in Gibeon, to the north.

Saul is a tragic case study of what happens when we suppose believers can succeed by adapting to society's standards and structures tooled for "success." Israel's carnal quest for a king . . . the whole confused perspective on how spiritual power is applied to life . . . Saul's final, disastrous battle after consulting a sorceress for counsel . . .; Saul was the victim of the same fallacy that has brought the downfall of innumerable hearts, homes and hopes—even whole congregations. It is the fallacy that

God can be manipulated or that human enterprise can somehow add to the glory of God's purposes among His people.

But now David had ascended the throne. Saul was dead, and everything that had characterized his morally inconsistent and spiritually barren rule was beginning to be reversed. David, sensing that the presence of the living God is the only true source of abiding, abounding blessing, asked, "How can the ark of the Lord come to me?" (2 Samuel 6:9). One can hear his heart cry out, "I want God to live where I live!" Thus, asking, "Come dwell among us," David invited the presence of God back into the life of a nation. He knew full well that the Ark's return was not the recovery of some talisman of good fortune or a treasured gold box filled with antiques to be venerated. Rather, David knew the Ark was linked with God's presence because of God's commitment to the word of His covenant. He perceived that where people loved God and His Word, the testimony of His faithfulness would focus in glory and benediction upon them! Be sure of this: David wanted God, not just success!

Though his motives were flawless, however, what David did next is hard to understand.

He built a cart.

His apparent purpose was to transport the Ark in style, and to bring "the glory" to Jerusalem in a way that would befit the worthiness of the Lord. A cart may have seemed like a good idea since the Philistines had used one to transport it to its current location. It is an almost humorous commentary on the way the Church, or any of us as sincere believers, will resort to the "world mind" without recognizing it. It doesn't work—not then, not now.

David, emulating heathen action without intending it, ended in paying a sore price in this misguided attempt at trying to "move God": *death*. A man helping to transport the Ark died instantly while attempting to steady it on the cart.

It all seems so unfair. ("I mean, we tried so hard.") But the lesson readily drawn from David's abortive effort at welcoming the Lord to his house is that God never comes to us on man's terms—only on His own. This event does not reflect an unwillingness or mercilessness on God's part; rather, it emphasizes our own need to be in appropriate and wise alignment with His ways.

Thus it was that David discovered one of God's ways: The Ark did not travel on carts, but on the shoulders of praising priests and among people who worship His way. And the message distilled for us: God's entry to our "house" never comes by human systems or formulas, but by our intimate, humble openness to Him.

Let's capture these lessons:

- See David's *hunger* for God's presence—a real and passionate quest for His work in his life (2 Samuel 6:9).

- See David's *teachability*—his willingness to be corrected and to learn the Lord's ways of doing things (1 Chronicles 15:15–24).

- See David's *humility* as he abandons pride with childlike rejoicing, evidence that he is more impressed with God's glory than with his own (2 Samuel 6:16, 21–22).

These three qualities—hunger for God, teachableness by God and humility before God—are foundational to bringing home the glory. Once these qualifications are met, life begins to spring forth and the meaning in God's attendant glory is manifest: God's *protection* and *direction* begin to be provided at broad dimensions. David's rule is not only secured by glory; it begins to be advanced mightily. (Ensuing episodes confirm this; see 2 Samuel 8, especially verse 6.)

Although no physical manifestation of glory ever occurred during David's lifetime—no smoke, cloud, mist or fire pillar—a continuing succession of events verified the presence of God's glory and blessing. As Isaiah's prophecy later expressed it, the glory will be for a covering (4:5). So David experienced it in his time. He models a potential that continues into the present, providing "cover" and defining the meaning of God's presence in glory for all time.

The idea behind "covering" isn't mysterious at all. The covering glory cloud and pillar of fire in ancient Israel's wilderness journeys accomplished two things: They both led the way (Exodus 40:36–37) and guarded it (Exodus 14:19–20).

The same is ours today, since the promise for every dwelling and assembly to be attended by God's glory has been prophesied with promise! God holds forth to each of us the hope of both divine direction and protection. Now the real power inherent in His glory when it comes to our house waits to be ministered.

Ministering "in the Glory"

We have been careful to repeat that inviting God's glory home is not simply for the sake of our enjoying some private mystical experience. Neither is it for building a shrine or claiming some unique superiority of spiritual attainment. *Applied glory,* if you will, is practical. It involves moving into prayer and "extending the boundaries of God's blessing" through the privilege of His power entrusted to you and me by faith.

Moses led the people *forward* under the glory cloud.

David *expanded* Israel's boundaries through victories given him through and for God's glory.

In the same way, people of the glory need to understand the ministry of the glory. Just as the ministry of praise and worship welcomes God's glory, the ministry of prayer applies it to actual circumstances. It applies the fruit of praise in faith.

Dolores, a member of our congregation, tells how God began to deal with her and her husband about their neighborhood. Repeatedly, as she rose to pray mornings, the phrase *Stretch out your boundaries* came to her. She was stirred while reading Isaiah 54: "Lengthen your cords, and strengthen your stakes. For you shall expand to the right and to the left" (verses 2–3). Examining the whole of that chapter, she found a number of benefits included in "stretching out your boundaries":

- Blessings upon her children ("your descendants will inherit the nations"—verse 3b);

- The possibility of re-peopling places like her own city, desolated by sin, with inhabitants who honor God (verse 3c);

- Banishing the shameful things of the past, since God wants to bless people (verse 4a); and

- The transformation of "disgraced" people and circumstances by reason of God's intervention (verse 4b).

Dolores perceived these spiritual insights as promptings from God toward regular prayer over her neighborhood. Shortly after this, she and her husband started to pray regularly for the boundaries of God's blessing to extend from her house—to "crowd back the darkness" around them. Without telling anyone, they began to take frequent walks around the block, interceding for their neighborhood and the people who lived there.

1. They prayed that the Lord would soften people's hearts to receive Him.

2. They prayed that God would put them in contact with people they could help, and people to whom they could give a true witness of who Jesus really is.

3. They prayed that people who had hardened their hearts against God and His working would move to another neighborhood.

4. They prayed for God's peace and protection over their area of the city.

5. They prayed for neighborhood businesses to recognize their prosperity as God's blessing on them.

As Dolores and her husband continued interceding over an extended period of time, the Holy Spirit gradually prompted them to enlarge the area over which they prayed until it measured to about eleven square blocks. Then they began to notice several signs that the Lord was honoring their obedience. They were able to lead several neighbors to the Lord. They were allowed to share with some of the business people that they had prayed for them regularly—a fact that, due to the credibility of this couple, was very moving to some of those leaders.

It began to seem there were more believers everywhere! Bumper stickers about the Lord began to appear, testifying to a change of constituency. A local pastor who did not bear a living testimony of Jesus Christ was replaced by a Spirit-filled pastor who began to lead the flock with godly influence. Consequently, the day school at that church began to change as children and teens were impacted by the new pastor's life.

This couple felt no smugness about the changes being effected in their part of town, as though they were secret practitioners of some magical art. They simply knew that through prayer, God's "glory on their house" was a transmittable dynamic; their prayers were transforming their neighborhood.

One of their most satisfying moments came in casual conversation with a next-door neighbor whose remark one day touched them: "You know, I can't really explain it. It just seems to me like our neighborhood is starting to feel different—genuinely *good*. Have you noticed anything like this?" God had taken the lips of a person who knew nothing of their prayer pursuit and had testified to them of the fruit of their faith. Dolores and her husband are a study in "applied glory."

So is a person we'll call Norman. He learned something of applied glory at that point of one's "house" we've cited as *responsibility*. This is what happened right on the job amid his daily occupation.

The whole community was stunned. Very few favored what had been done. But certain theaters had chosen to run the film "The Last Temptation of Christ." You probably remember the nationwide outcry when that motion picture was released. Norman was one of the multitudes of Christians offended by that crude depiction of Jesus concocted in a gross miscarriage of what was being called creative license. Many sincere believers were conducting organized marches on theaters and other crusade tactics, while on the other side "censorship" was being screamed. In the middle, a Christian was faced with a unique challenge.

Peculiarly enough, Norman was executive assistant to a primary stockholder in the movie. While this didn't affect Norman's work (since the man's interests did not flavor Norman's own testimony in working where he did), the furor over the film did create a stressed situation.

The angered executive was becoming more and more incensed at "the mindless emotional display of these [expletive deleted] Christians!" There were times in the office that the air was blue. Not only did Norman feel bad that his sin-blinded boss was party to the blasphemous production, but he hated the verbal blasphemy filling the office as reports increased of Christian protests.

Norman was not too cowardly to register public protest himself, but knew nothing would be gained by that—not with his boss, anyway. Nor did he fear losing his job if he spoke up. Rather, he sought a more penetrating way to transform the situation than bringing political or economic pressure.

Being part of a congregation in which people had learned the principles of praise and prayer as weapons for evicting the operations of hell's demonic enterprise, Norman took a different tack. The morning after a particularly violent explosion of anger by his boss, Norman went to the office early. Moving through the boss's office, he began to pray and praise, doing three things in particular:

- He *declared* the authority of the name of Jesus Christ above the spirits of profanity and blasphemy.

- He *allowed* the Holy Spirit's overflow to fill the room with God's love, inviting the Lord to supplant the hatred and anger with His sanity and order.

- He *invited* the glory of God to overrule and cast down the works of the flesh and the devil.

Here is Norman's own description of how the office changed:

"*Not once* after I prayed," he rejoiced, "were there the blasphemous outbursts that had been occurring; and within a matter of hours, my boss invited me into conference with him. 'Norm, you know I've been infuriated by all the stir over this film. I know you're a devout Christian, and I'd like to ask your help.'

"From there," Norman continued, "my boss asked my insight as to exactly what it was that was angering the Christians. Amazingly, without the help our conversation brought, he actually couldn't see the issue through the eyes of hurt and offended believers in Jesus. But now he listened. Further, he asked my recommendations on things that might improve relations with the Christian community. The staggering fact is that these men, without any real knowledge of the Lord or His Word, truly believed that what they were trying to present might help people incline toward spiritual values. They couldn't imagine how it could be seen as an attack on Christianity."

Some people may feel that Norman's response wasn't assertive enough or that he lacked a tougher, more activist approach. But Norm's actions did align with Jesus' words:

> "Love your enemies, bless those who curse you, do
> good to those who hate you, and pray for those who
> spitefully use you and persecute you, that you may
> be sons of your Father in heaven. . . ."
>
> Matthew 5:44–45

Although his boss never knew why, the situation changed almost overnight. Norman's explanation helped the boss and his associates come to an accountable understanding of their actions. Communications between the owners and the public began to take place. Tensions faded and threats ceased. While the film didn't disappear, its impact was reduced radically. Peace began to permeate the situation because one of God's "glory" people had acted.

This is not to say, of course, that every improvement resulted from Norman's actions alone. Nor can we say that everything turned out ideally, or that every time believers take such action they will have that quick a response. Until Christ returns and ultimately banishes the works of darkness, such circumstances will continue. We live in a world the Bible describes as dominated by "the god of this age, who blinds the minds of those who do not believe" (2 Corinthians 4:4, paraphrase).

Nonetheless, this darkened world and the darkened minds in it can be penetrated by people who learn how to both bring the glory home and apply it to their whole "house."

But what if *you* find *your* house tinged with darkness? Is it possible to apply glory when *you* are living in a shadow?

4

Cleansing a "Leprous" House

Can a house be possessed, oppressed or burdened with a history that stifles its future? I think so.

The "house" assigned to me when I took that small pastorate in Van Nuys had originally been dedicated to the worship of God, and I was convinced of and committed to that priority. I wanted God to move among us and for us to gather in the spirit of praise, welcoming His workings in our midst.

Still, the spirit of our gatherings (well before the visitation of glory) was less than fully satisfying, and I was yet to learn a whole skein of lessons that would alter my perspective on the spiritual realm. These lessons might prove worthwhile to you, for they don't apply only to church-houses. They fit the setting of any house that anyone hopes to see filled with glory.

At the beginning the spirit of praise in our services was not generated easily. If I had not learned to take a strong stance and contend against the nagging, systematically present sense of praiselessness, we would have withered on the vine.

It wasn't that our little congregation was resistant. That small group of dear people had an extended history of worshiping God openly and expressively—some as many as fifty years. But no tradition is a guarantee of dynamic; and looking back, I believe most of them would admit that their praise, though sincere, had become perfunctory and programmed.

The barrenness of holy habit unaccompanied by holy fire is a threat to us all. Sincerity notwithstanding, any people can fall into the trap Jesus addressed: "This people honors Me with their lips, but their heart is far from Me. And in vain they worship Me."[1] The *function* of worship without *fire* in worship prevents the release of *fragrance* in worship. The incense of the soul is trapped inside where neither God nor man can rejoice in its fullness and beauty.

The problem in our case, however, was not something needing to be added; and it was entrenched far more deeply than simply in a human disposition.

Quite apart from any lack of vitality among the people themselves, a strange and oppressive atmosphere seemed to "possess" the building's sanctuary. This was more than a matter of aesthetics. The "feel" of the place had nothing to do with the simplicity of the building itself—a simple one modeled after a World War II Army base chapel, rustic and inviting.

There was a cold clamminess about it, much like the quenching effect a manic-depressive personality can bring into a room. The members themselves would sometimes comment on the heaviness, if not the gloom. It almost seemed as though a personality resided in that room, intent on hindering free, wholehearted worship within those walls. I knew it was not my imagination.

Still, when other people mentioned it, I usually passed over their observation, preferring to avoid anything that could engender either negativity or superstition.

The "Leprous House"

There is an unusual passage in Leviticus that most of us simply glide by when reading through this ritual-filled book of Mosaic ordinances. But here, in the very center of it all (14:33–57), the Lord instructed the people of Israel in the proper way to cleanse a house contaminated with leprosy. I would later come to see the practical wisdom of the text for today. Circumstances change, after all, but the wisdom of the Word is timeless.

It is not considered mysterious to believe that *physical* infection may remain in a dwelling. All kinds of precautions are taken by the medical community to disinfect and protect against the transmission of disease through objects or uncleansed rooms. It does, on the other hand, sometimes seem strange to think of a *spiritual* malady or presence lingering and infecting a physical object or location.

I was unwilling to dismiss the heaviness in that place as illusory. I did not yet realize either the full dimension of the biblical basis for my concern or the spiritual solution to it. But I felt determined not to surrender to what Isaiah describes as a "spirit of heaviness."[2] Although I did not yet know exactly what was wrong nor how to deal with it, I knew this house needed cleaning. And when it was all over, I had learned the lesson of cleansing the leprous house.

Although this is a new concept to some of us, its roots are ancient, grounded by God in the Old Testament.

In Leviticus 13–14, Moses gave the regulations for purification from leprosy, that hideously deforming disease that rots away the flesh and is so frighteningly infectious. The ease with which this vicious affliction can be transmitted lay behind the concern shown in the Law. But as practical as the guidelines may seem in Leviticus 14:33–53 for dealing with the cleansing of a human body, they include instructions for cleansing a leprous house. It is that turn from personal leprosy to the Lord's concern about buildings that first catches our surprise: "A building with leprosy?!"

It is clear that in some instances the text refers only to an apparent infestation of natural fungus. But even though there is nothing "spiritual" in that, the Lord directed the Israelites not only to meet the obvious need for cleansing the house physically with plain old soap and water, but to apply spiritual dynamics in housecleaning as well. The purification ritual involved both a physical and a spiritual application, showing that houses even then could be polluted at both levels—a physical level of infectious filth and a level of spiritual infestation, too.

This is not a matter of superstition.

I feel no hesitation asserting the potential of such a problem today since even historic Bible commentators do so.

First, it is true, as the *Cambridge Bible* says, that certain of the leprous infestations "were due to damp or decay, or the growth of some vegetable matter."[3] The first segment of the Levitical text on this matter, therefore, directed the normal cleansing process (verses 33–42). But more severe situations identified "an *active* leprosy in the house" (verse 44, literally "bad or angry"). Here, it seems, even in the middle of what might appear to point only to judicious hygienic principles in one's dwelling, God's Word signals something more sinister.

Remember, Israel was inheriting dwelling places formerly inhabited by a people whose lifestyle was evil, corrupted by violent forms of immoral, idolatrous worship, including the sacrificing of their children to demons. In reference to this passage in Leviticus, the renowned Lutheran scholars Kiel and Delitzch write,

> The only thing that can be gathered from the signs mentioned is that the house-leprosy was an evil. . . . For, although it is primarily in the human body that sin manifests itself, it spreads from man to the things which he touches, uses, inhabits, though without our being able to represent this spread as a physical contagion.[4]

John Gill, the classic Puritan preacher, wrote concerning this text: "This house may be an emblem of a visible church of God on earth which is often in scripture compared to a house, or that which signifies both an edifice and a family. . . ." Gill goes on to describe the dynamic polluting effects of sin's infectious power.[5]

While none of these writers means to advance superstitious notions, neither do they hesitate to suggest that this infectious condition in the dwelling places inherited by the Israelites was without significant spiritual implications. Why was God so concerned with this housecleaning? Perhaps the rabbis themselves provide us with the answer. In the *Soncino Chumanh,* a scholarly work serving the Jewish spiritual community, Rabbi Cohen's comments on Leviticus 14 note:

According to the Midrash [rabbinical commentaries], the Amorites concealed treasures of gold in the walls of their houses during the forty years of Israel's wanderings in the wilderness, in order that when the Israelites conquered the land they would not be able to lay their hands on these valuables. God, therefore, smote the houses with the plague that the Israelites should demolish them and so discover the hidden treasure.[6]

This brings us more closely to the issue, and probably explains the strange words in which the Lord says *He* is the one who "put the leprous plague in a house" (verse 34). *God put it there!* Why?

It appears that the Lord was taking action to expose the presence of a deeper evil. By compelling a physical manifestation of its presence to surface—"an active leprosy"—God was pointing His people toward identifying an infectious source of evil that could pollute their dwelling, and thus pointing toward its removal.

Consider this fact. Most of the precious items of gold, silver and valuable stones treasured by the Canaanite and Amorite peoples were handcrafted by pagan artists, virtually all of whom featured the gods and goddesses of their demon deity system in most of their work. The artists themselves were committed communicators of the corroded values of their culture. Thus, in some houses, the objects "hidden in the walls," as noted above, were actually objects dedicated to the worship of satanic beings!

Small wonder, then, that God was unwilling to allow any residue of the former occupants to infect the house of His own people. His act of "putting a leprosy" on the house was no arbitrary action. Instead, it was His means of exposing the corrupt system those things represented in the invisible realm, forcing the visible manifestation of their decadence, expressing their corrosiveness in actual physical evidence.

The rabbinic idea of "treasures in the wall" may not answer all the questions, but it is believable that on some occasions God was helping His people by pointing out the presence of evil. It wasn't to make them wealthy but to keep them healthy. Any such objects removed would not—*could not!*—be retained by the individual anyway. Deuteronomy 7:23–26, 13:16 and Joshua 7–8 show that these objects were to be submitted to the corporate leadership and destroyed by fire. If anything of worth remained, it belonged to the Lord.

In any case, the "house leprosy" the Israelites encountered was not to be taken casually or without specific action. The action God directed is still instructive: "Make atonement for the house" (Leviticus 14:53). Notice that the solution is not merely hygienic; it is spiritual as well, employing redemptive action.

The issue required the power of God's sacrificial system. It was a priority to rid the house of what was so real and potentially destructive in the invisible realm that its power was manifested in the physical realm. Such a leprosy had to be dealt with by spiritual redemption. So it was that sacrifice was offered. Elaborate detail is given to this, and appropriately so, for each facet forecasts a different aspect of the ultimate sacrifice of Jesus on the cross. The application of that sacrificial testimony, applied to the dwelling through the worship of the occupant, was lifted to God in obedient faith. And the net result: "[The house] shall be clean" (Leviticus 14:53)!

Breaking the Stronghold

We have been examining this issue because what may to the casual reader appear to be a peculiar command of God to those who invaded Canaan 3,400 years ago actually holds significant insight for us today. We are at the very least instructed by analogy. Cleansing from leprosy illustrates other kinds of cleansings.

But I believe we are dealing with more than an interesting parallel. I think God was speaking in this passage directly to the fact that the spiritual and the physical are not so much two different realms as two integrated realities. We all live in direct touch with both. The problem is, the majority of us learn to live life only with reference to the physical realm. God wants us to learn to be as effective in one facet of life as the other; to know, in other words, how to deal with the *real* world, all of it.

Spiritually unclean things, when given place to, *do* rot. The spiritually corrupt may take on a spiritual dimension that can dwell in our homes, our cars, our offices, our work, our school lockers—anyplace over which we have been given dominion.

So it was with the sanctuary of the church at the time Anna and I came to Van Nuys. The fact that such an oppressing presence had gained a place is no commentary on the people or the leaders preceding me. It is, however, a reminder of how subtly the adversary worms his way into situations where, if recognized, he would be entirely unwelcome. Nor would I have realized the source or nature of that discouraging "clamminess" but for the Holy Spirit's signal.

So it was one afternoon, a number of weeks after assuming the pastorate, that I stopped near the front of the sanctuary in the area surrounding the altar. For the slightest moment I saw something. *Or did I?* I asked myself.

Like any rational person, I am reticent to acknowledge "seeing" things, so I peered up into the rafters that formed the visible support system for the room. *Yes,* I confirmed to myself, *there is something there.* A small, dark, cloudlike object seemed to be. . . .

But it's gone now.

I was puzzled, but only for a moment. Within seconds, and without words being spoken to my mind, I was "taught." At least that is how I would describe what I believe the Holy Spirit did for me in that instance. I was taught:

1. There *is* a presence, and its source is satanic.

2. Its mission is to oppress the Father's work here.

3. You need not fear it or speak to anyone about it.

4. Simply set yourself in steadfast praise: It cannot win.

And that is what I began to do.

Most important, I feel, is the fact that I did not speak to others about it. Sometimes people receive insight about Satan's workings but speak too readily about it, only advancing his effectiveness rather than neutralizing it. Too few of the Lord's people are familiar enough with God's Word to hear of such things without becoming either frightened and distracted, or else preoccupied with a bizarre interest in the demonic.

There is no question in my mind that the Holy Spirit's gift of discerning that spirit's operation in our midst was intended to strengthen my resolve, to further my pursuit of enriching worship in the Body life of the congregation and to summon my private intercession with faith.

And so I began.

Several times each week I made a point of walking through the sanctuary when no one else was there. Each time I did, I would lift my voice, shout the praises of God and clap my hands, declaring the glory and honor of our Lord Jesus Christ. I rejoiced in the Spirit and with singing, with a sense of commitment to praise God in defiance of whatever made the place so gloomy spiritually.

Through this kind of spiritual declaration and combat, joined to our corporate steadfastness in praise (while I *never* made public mention of the "cloud" or "clammy presence"), we eventually realized a victory over that spirit of heaviness. I am further convinced that the eventual visitation of glory was directly related to the earlier eviction of the dark, occupying presence that was attempting to restrict the faith, worship and joy in the flock.

The crisis in the struggle against that oppressive spirit took place, interestingly enough, on a Reformation Sunday in October. On a day celebrating the Church's breakthrough from historic religious bondage, we ourselves realized unexpected victory.

One of the congregation brought a prophetic word, spoken graciously and perfectly in order, exhorting that we should praise the Lord. We were about fifteen minutes into the service when it was given. But a bewildering thing happened: No one did or said anything in response. I had expected the people to respond with upraised hands and voices, lifting praise to the Lord. But nothing happened.

I hardly knew what to do. I was reluctant to speak up

because a number of visitors were present. (Sadly, every pastor is tempted from time to time to make the church "look good" to visitors.) If I confronted the congregation's unresponsiveness on the spot now, it could disturb the smooth flow of the service.

But then and there I made a lifetime decision. I decided I would never again condition any response to God's dealings with a concern about pleasing man. It was a crucially important moment.

I came down from the pulpit area, stood in front of the congregation—about one hundred were present—and said, "First, I want to say to any who are visiting that I hope you will not be uncomfortable by what I am going to say. Please understand my desire to make you feel welcome, but at the same time I must, as pastor of this flock, speak a few words of correction."

Then I changed my tone, not to accuse but to express my pain.

"Church, do you realize what we have just done? God, by His Holy Spirit, has just called us in a beautiful and gracious way to praise Him for His great love and goodness to us, and we have responded with silence. I know neither you nor I want to disobey the Word or the Spirit of God, so let's make a decision together, right now. We're going to stop everything and give ourselves to worship and praise until together we sense that we have responded adequately to God's call to worship."

And we did.

We stood and sang several songs of praise. After that we worshiped, speaking forth the glories of the Lord. And in the next few minutes, the room seemed to brighten— not visibly, but in a way that anyone present could tell we had done the right thing.

That same evening, as the congregation was singing a series of hymns, I turned to the pastoral staff member seated beside me on the platform.

"Chuck," I exclaimed, "a tremendous spirit of joy and liberty is here tonight."

He smiled his agreement, nodding his head and continuing to sing along with the people. I dismissed the matter from my mind. But God wasn't through teaching me.

The following Tuesday, as I drove home following my lecture at LIFE Bible College, the strongest impression filled my mind: *The reason for the liberty you experienced Sunday is that the hold of the spirit that has oppressed the church here has been broken.*

I knew it was the Holy Spirit's word to me, and my spirit leaped! I began to smile to myself. Something wonderful had taken place and my heart was gladdened. The same gladness has continued upon the countenance of our congregation ever since that stronghold of resistance was broken. Praise and worship have flowed freely ever since.

Years later, in relating this story, the text of Leviticus 14 came forcefully back to me. I realized we had been dealing with a spiritual leprosy manifesting itself through a spirit of heaviness and oppression. While everything seemed right and in order about our lives before the Lord (and, in fact, was right), the physical dwelling of our congregation needed to be purged and presented to Him anew.

Further study convinced me that the cleansing principles of Leviticus 14 are equally applicable to our private homes, just as they were with ancient Israel. And I became convinced that spiritual leprosy can come to dwell in a place for many different reasons.

As I said earlier, I am not attempting to prove that God's Word says demons were attached to the leprosy or fungus in the houses Israel inherited. Neither can I propose conclusively that what Israel did was a means to rid their houses of some sinister spiritual power. The Bible does say, however, that the things Israel experienced are intended to be examples understood and applied by us who live in the last times.[7] Further, we are shown that the last times will be a uniquely oppressive demon-filled era. The term *perilous times* about which Paul warns in 2 Timothy 3:1 specifically means "vicious, lion-like."

In the light of Peter's counsel, that our adversary prowls continually like a lion to seek a place of advantage over us, the issue is settled: We are in an arena of spiritual control and combat. We are wise, therefore, to recognize—not with fear, but by being strengthened in faith—that our day is one of distinct conflict. It calls for the disciplines of spiritual wisdom to dominate our lifestyle.

Purging and Praise

The example in Leviticus shows the wisdom of "cleansing" your homes. Although the rituals described may sound foreign, and even though everything they prefigured by Old Testament type has been fulfilled in Christ, they present principles for practical application today. Most specific are the principles of *purging* and *praise*.

The scraping of the house walls described in the leprous house text applies the first principle of *purging* through either the removal of the unworthy or the physical cleaning of the dwelling. The ensuing sacrifice that was offered demonstrates the second principle of *praise,* which today is applied with our lips, our actions, our songs and our worship, inviting the presence of God directly into our home. Both principles are applied on the grounds of Christ's victory through the cross and both bring about a clean house.

Let me tell another story. A young couple assuming their first church pastorate experienced a remarkable case of the power of purging and praise to transform a situation. They had been asked to accept a small church in central California that had just undergone the upheaval of immorality. A disastrous fall had resulted from temptation that had seized the previous pastor and then ripped the soul of the whole congregation. Blinded by an infatuation, a good man had been deceived by the devil, divorced his wife, left with one of the women in the congregation and thrown the entire church into confusion and shock. The young pair recognized it would be an incredible challenge just to hold the congregation and reinstate unity, let alone deal with the demands of learning, as they themselves were new to pastoral leadership.

Upon their arrival, they made a confounding discovery. Every pastor who had ministered in that building since it had been built had left because of the same problem: immorality. Even though the place had belonged to several different denominations, this one horrible common denominator remained. The young couple were wise enough to recognize they were up against a principality of long standing, one that would like to make them yet another casualty in the spiritual battle.

Then, as they were moving into the house they had

rented, since the church had no parsonage, the landlady remarked to the young pastor's wife that every couple who had ever rented that house had moved out because they were getting a divorce. "You're such a nice family," she said. "I almost hate to see you move in here."

They went to prayer with a two-pronged focus. They felt that the congregation needed to continue to be led in worship until the spirit afflicting them was broken—*praising*. They also felt they were to cleanse their home—*purging*.

This second conviction took a very practical turn. They spent an entire month cleaning that house—every ceiling, wall, light, shelf, nook and cranny. They also cleaned every one of their own belongings—every piece of furniture, china, linen, etc. In essence, they were making a statement: Nothing unclean will be tolerated here! They saw themselves as taking a stand in the spiritual realm by what they were doing in the natural. By the end of that month, everything in that home had been cleaned, purged.

The result? They remained in that pastorate for three years, saw the church recover and experience fruitful growth. And—hallelujah!—they were the first couple ever to leave a pastorate in that building with their marriage intact and flourishing!

A House for the Lord

The cleansing of our homes by no means always involves confronting the demonic. Sometimes the problem is flesh, not spirit. Just as surely as the Bible calls us to present our bodies to our living Lord in worship,[8] we are equally called to ensure that our dwellings are Christ-worthy. We are admonished, "Be not conformed to this world."[9]

But living in today's culture can deaden our sensitivities like a devilish shot of novocaine. Too easily we become numb to the spiritual erosion sucking the ground from beneath us. Standing on the Rock of Christ Jesus and the Word of God are the only sure foundations for a house that will survive.

What steps can we take to live out that lifestyle?

First, fill your house with worship: "Present your bodies a living sacrifice, and be transformed by the renewing of your mind." Present your body, daily and literally, to the Lord in worship. Stand or kneel or lift your hands, not as a ritual performance but as a demonstration statement. In some way each day, rise to present your body in praise to Him. You will find this to be more than a set of calisthenics. Your mind will begin to function differently, for our mind turns toward what our body is given to.

So begin with worship. I often suggest to people that before anything else occurs in a day, they bow to their knees. Not for an extended time, for this first-thing-on-rising is not intended to substitute for one's devotional life. But in those opening seconds of a new day, slip to your knees and say, "Lord, this day is Yours, and so am I." Declare His authority over all your life for all this day; then rise and be about your regimen.

Second, assess the details of your life. A leprous house may be the raw result of having neglected practical principles for wholeness in living with Jesus Christ. Here is a set of seven thoughts to consider in assessing your own life. They are not meant as a rigid set of laws but as a healthy set of guidelines.

1. Have you compromised anywhere in your choice of friends or activities?

Ephesians 5:11 tells us to "have no fellowship with the unfruitful works of darkness, but rather expose them." First Corinthians 5:9 adds that we are not to keep company with immoral people. These verses don't give us license to judge self-righteously or reject a brother or sister in Christ who has failed. The intent, rather, is that we not nurture a relationship with a person sloppy about promiscuity or committed to a pattern of ongoing sin. This is not a matter of self-righteous snobbishness but practical Christlikeness.[10]

"But didn't Jesus eat with sinners and prostitutes?" someone protests.

Yes. The Bible does not direct us away from the unconverted who need our touch with the life and love of Jesus. We are appointed as salt in the midst of that world and light in the midst of that darkness. Like Jesus we are to touch their lives, minister His understanding, reveal His care and love them into life.

But we are not to be *entangled* with them. "Be not unequally yoked together with unbelievers" does not refer only to marriage; it relates to all our associations, from friendships to business relationships. Let's not confuse our availability to witness with an acceptance of worldliness!

2. Do you maintain obedience to parents?

Romans 1:28–32 outlines a stark list of the things that pervade the world and destroy societies. Some tend to review that list and notice only the words against sexual perversion. But notice that disobedience to parents is right there, too, sounding almost tame compared to some other things listed.

Yet we parents need to recognize that requiring obedience of our children is our responsibility. It is as much a part of keeping our homes clear of the perversity in the world as worship is. In every home, biblical discipline accompanied by love, teaching and understanding secure a pathway to life for the children and health in the home!

The Bible says that parents who do not reprove their children are paving the way for hell to master those children (Proverbs 23:14). Homes that tolerate disobedience to parents become leprous; family life putrefies and children rot.

3. Do you participate in any lying, dishonesty or untruthfulness?

"Do not lie to one another, since you have put off the old man with his deeds" (Colossians 3:9). I am amazed by the number of people who think a lie is only deceiving words. The fact is, the spirit of deception invades in many ways. The Holy Spirit has a way of keeping us honest if we let Him. He is the Spirit of truth and will keep all manner of compromise *out* if He is allowed rule *within*— our hearts and our homes. Any untruthfulness is unworthy of a place in "my place."[11]

4. Do you exercise impure joking or speech?

The conscience of the culture around us is becoming more seared every day, and we are all vulnerable to becoming desensitized. The profusion of profanity surrounding us makes it no longer "shocking." Have you seen a movie recently or rented a video and found that the foul language did not assault your senses? The Scriptures admonished believers in a culture like ours to put away all evil speaking (Ephesians 4:31). The same goes today. Let's make David's cry our own: "Let the words of my mouth and the meditation of my heart be acceptable in Your sight, O Lord, my strength and my redeemer" (Psalm 19:14).

5. Do you sample or practice any known disobedience?

With substance abuse rampant, some sincere believers are duped by false notions of grace. Issues like smoking, drinking, marijuana and pills raise questions for many. And so they should, for the Bible says our bodies are the temples of the Holy Spirit. So what about our houses?

Nothing in the Bible ties our eternal salvation to these practices, so I do not raise the issue to threaten the immoderate Christian with hell. Our salvation is not so thin or shallow that it cannot survive the physically and psychologically corrosive effects of indulgence or tragic points of personal bondage.

However—and let it be *strongly* asserted!—we are wise to remember our accountability as stewards of what God has given us. Real deliverance from binding habits flows only from true repentance and bold renunciation. Pat Robertson tells the story of his own conversion and sudden awareness that liquor was to have no more place in his life. "I poured a huge bottle of expensive Scotch whiskey right down the drain," he wrote. He knew it was to have no power over his life, and he demonstrated his commitment and newfound liberty by taking house-cleansing action.

6. Have you given astrology or occult practices any place at all?

Often people who have come to know Christ do so from a past involving occult practices. Sometimes they keep some paraphernalia or books, not realizing that the presence of such things in the home does matter. Just as the book of Deuteronomy commanded the burning of what characterized the old society, so Acts 19:18–20 relates a similar episode in the New Testament Church. Men and women being born again in Ephesus, where the occult abounded, brought together all occult materials and burned them.

Other items may have been brought home as gifts or souvenirs that are attended by an evil related to their derivation. There are no hard and fast rules about this, and I am not going to advise you exactly what you should or should not throw away. But the Holy Spirit will if you will allow Him to. Walk through your house with Him and ask Him to show you what to do. Even when something leprous has been brought into the home innocently, it still needs to be purged.

7. What about the pornographic or obscene?

Music, literature, pictures, phone calls—all surround us in wide availability. It is ignorance to suppose that idolatry is simply bowing to wooden or stone figurines, and that it is but a practice of ancient history. Since most of the ancient religions used perverse sexual activity as part of their worship ritual, their "gods" were actually pornographic figures. Artifacts verify this, some of them absolutely foul and debasing in their projection of human sensuality. The only difference today is the ability of our culture to craft the idols; pornographic videos, books and pictures are all "bowed unto" by too many believers who wonder why their homes, families, jobs and influence seem unhealthy or withering. There's no mystery about it: Leprosy is in their house.

The Calvary "Covering"

However one assesses ways in which leprosy may infest a house, the consummate point of focus should always be the cross of Jesus. The apostle Paul made this clear when he called the early Corinthians to a housecleaning of all their life and living. He employed as his analogy the ancient Israeli Feast of Unleavened Bread:

> Therefore purge out the old leaven [yeast], that you may be a new lump [of bread dough], since you truly are unleavened [i.e., cleansed through salvation].
>
> For indeed Christ, our Passover, was sacrificed for us. Therefore let us keep the feast, not with old leaven [i.e., old ways and habits], nor with the leaven of malice and wickedness, but with the unleavened bread of sincerity and truth.
>
> 1 Corinthians 5:7–8

The picture is a powerful one, drawn from that unforgettable day when Israel was delivered from slavery in Egypt. The blood of the Passover lamb had both protected and released them, sparing them the judgment coming on the land and occasioning the circumstance that forced Pharaoh's edict to let them go. Into this dramatic deliverance the Holy Spirit has threaded a truth we are wise to remember.

Even as the children of Israel rejoiced in the new life of freedom unfolding before them through God's love and power, they were called to establish an annual feast in conjunction with the Passover remembrance. They were not only to commemorate their deliverance, but be reminded that they were called to a new lifestyle as well. "No leaven shall be found in your houses," said the Lord.[12] The annual weeklong observance of yeast-free eating was a reminder that their tastes were not to be dictated by their past. It is a fact that no previous society in the ancient world had cultivated the art of baking and the use of yeast as the Egyptians had. The message is clear: God was not condemning baked goods, but calling His redeemed to cease being controlled by society's "tastes," and to be freed from any domination of their own habits by sense-centered drives.

And they were pointed to the Passover.

Here, towering above all, was the annual celebration *in their houses* of the reminder that it was in their homes and over their families that God had provided the Passover lamb to secure their present and their future. The New Testament is crystal-clear as to the specific meaning of the Passover for the believer in Jesus: "Behold! The Lamb of God, who takes away the sin of the world!"[13] It is Jesus' shed blood and substitutionary death on the cross that is our sole hope of salvation. And that same power is our sole hope of having "glory" for a covering on our houses. Isaiah's prophecy of the glory is preceded by a condition: "When the Lord has washed away the filth of the daughters of Zion . . ." (4:4–6). The foundation for glory is the cross—and so is the hope for cleansing and providing a fresh covering for a leprous house. All the purifying actions in the world cannot supplant the ultimate means of sanctifying the house: claiming the power of the blood of the cross!

Anna and I learned this point of wisdom long ago. Having moved into a house where the preceding occupant had experienced great difficulty with a son addicted to drugs and afflicted with horrible flashbacks from his involvement in Vietnam, we encountered bewildering problems almost immediately. Sickness was the primary issue, since all four of our kids were having difficulties of every kind.

One evening about two weeks after moving, I was just about to lie down for the night when the Lord brought to my mind the truth about sanctifying a house by the blood of Jesus.

"You know, honey," I said to Anna, who was just preparing for the night herself, "I think there is something of a relationship between the kids' constant sickness since we moved here and the fact that this house was—I guess you might say 'infested' with bad things before."

Anna's response was instant: "Just today I was thinking that same thing."

We didn't need handwriting on the wall. The Lord had dealt with us both, and we took action.

We prepared the elements of the Lord's Table and went into the living room and partook of Communion together, with worship and praise to our Lord Jesus. As we did, we affirmed our trust in the power of His cross, not only for our salvation but for our complete covering of divine grace including health, strength and victory over all evil.

While I don't consider it necessary in order to receive those blessings, I chose to do something as a proclamation of faith. Anna and I stood at the front door of our house and touched the sideposts and the top of the doorframe with the grape juice, symbolizing the covering of Jesus' blood. I have no question that was already accomplished in prayer—but I *liked* doing it. I had the sense of standing with all who have staked their claim throughout history on "the blood of the Lamb and the word of their testimony." *They are the ones who overcome!*[14]

The next day we gathered our children together and told them what we had done the night before, and we re-celebrated Communion, this time with their involvement. We walked together as a family from room to room, declaring God's Word of blessing according to appropriate promises:

- In the bedrooms we recited the blessings of restful sleep: "I lay down and slept; I awoke, for the Lord sustained me" (Psalm 3:5) and "I will both lie down in peace, and sleep; for You alone, O Lord, make me dwell in safety" (Psalm 4:8).

- In the bathroom we declared the promises of health: "If you diligently heed the voice of the Lord your God and do what is right in His sight, give ear to His commandments and keep all His statutes, I will put none of the diseases on you which I have brought on the Egyptians. For I am the Lord who heals you" (Exodus 15:26).

- In the kitchen we expressed the promises of provision and strength: "So you shall serve the Lord your God, and He will bless your bread and your water. And I will take sickness away from the midst of you" (Exodus 23:25).

- In the living room we declared, "As for [us] and [our] house, we will serve the Lord" (Joshua 24:15), and we invited the Holy Spirit to fill our home and family life with the fullness of God's love and goodness.

- We even stood in the entry hall and prayed, "Lord, You have said You would bless our goings out and our comings in, and that if we acknowledge You in all our ways You will direct our paths."[15]

I probably don't need to add that the bewildering problems and persistent sickness in our home cleared up right away, demonstrating the power in the blood of Jesus.

Whatever the source of uncleanness, impurity, evil or carnality that infects and begets a leprous house, the answer is always and ultimately in the power of our Lord Jesus' cross.

Apply it.

Live under its covenant.

Experience its triumph.

And watch your children grow up as ours have—to do the same thing in establishing their own homes under the ultimate glory, the cross of Jesus!

Notes

[1] Mark 7:6–7; cf. Isaiah 29:13.

[2] Isaiah 61:3.

[3] Chapman and Streane, *The Cambridge Bible—Leviticus* (Cambridge University Press, 1914), pp. 83–84.

[4] C. F. Keil, *Commentary on Leviticus* (Grand Rapids: Eerdmans Publishing Co., 1978 printing), pp. 390–391.

[5] John Gill, *Commentary on Leviticus* (Grand Rapids: Baker Book House, 1980 reprint), pp. 491–493.

[6] A. Cohen, editor, *The Soncino Chumanh, Leviticus 14* (Jerusalem: Soncino Press, Ltd., 1983), p. 694.

[7] 1 Corinthians 10:11.

[8] Romans 12:1.

[9] Romans 12:2.

[10] 1 Corinthians 5:9–11.

[11] John 16:12,13; 1 John 4:6.

[12] Exodus 12:19.

[13] John 1:29.

[14] Revelation 12:11.

[15] Deuteronomy 28:6; Proverbs 3:6.

5

Doorposts of the Kingdom

It was a mild autumn evening as we gathered for prayer, just the four of us. Our pastoral staff does this customarily on Saturday evenings as we anticipate and welcome God's grace on another Sunday of worship and teaching. But on this particular night a most unusual thing took place—something that has forever affected my understanding of the importance of the spirit of praise and worship in inviting the presence of God's power in a "house."

As we were praying, I felt moved that we separate and go to the four corners of the sanctuary and extend our hands toward the middle of the room, as though we were lifting up a tent top formed by our extended arms. In fact, this command seemed somehow fixed in my mind: *Lift up a canopy*. I sensed that in some way our praises were providing a tabernacle-like dwelling place for the Lord's entry and visitation.

We did so. And as we began with prayerful praise, a most unique, distinct and pervading sense of God's presence filled the room. Time seemed to pass quickly as we

---

continued rejoicing in this marked sense of God's pleasure with our adoring praise. The event concluded without anything remarkable at the time, but more was to come—more of which we were yet unaware.

It was two weeks later as we gathered that I again felt this unusual prompting: *Go, stand at the room's four corners as before.*

I hesitated.

To my view, there is a certain wisdom to resisting doing anything just for its own sake, even more so if it might be a carnal or humanized attempt to "get a feeling." I discourage people, for example, from thinking they need always to sit at a certain place, or kneel a certain way, or pray with a specific tone of voice in order to contact God. Such habits smack of superstition, and are not characteristic of the creative, original ways in which the Holy Spirit works.

In my case, the impression was so strong that I overcame my natural hesitation, turned to the other fellows who were at prayer and apologized for interrupting, then explained. "I don't want to appear as though I'm trying to conjure up a feeling or establish some kind of tradition, but I think we're supposed to stand once again in praise at the four corners of the sanctuary." The men understood my attitude, and we each strolled to the separate corners of the large room, then turned to the center, facing one another. Shortly, we resumed prayer and praise as before.

It was only a few minutes later that our youth pastor stopped us. "Hey, guys," he said, "I don't know how this is going to sound to you, but I think the Lord just showed me something. Let me share it for your judgment because, even though it might sound strange, I really believe it's something the Lord just gave me." We all nodded in agreement, and listened as he continued.

"I think the Holy Spirit has shown me the reason it somehow seems so appropriate for us to stand as we are—here at the four corners of the building, worshiping the Lord in this way. He gave me a picture of four tall angelic beings stationed at the same places—the four corners; we are worshiping the Lord *with* them, in a kind of harmonizing of the visible and invisible realm."

None of us responded with unusual enthusiasm, but neither did we feel negative about what had been shared. We simply accepted what was spoken.

None of us knew of anything in the Scriptures that argued against what had been said. We were not being urged to worship the angels, which, of course, is entirely unscriptural (see Colossians 2:18; Revelation 19:10). Rather, if what had been expressed was really so, we were simply being encouraged to partner with worship that was already in progress, joining praises from earth with praises in heaven. It was an interesting thought, but for all of us—our youth leader included—it spoke nothing particularly clear to our understanding at the time. That is why I forgot the matter.

But about ten days after that evening a funny thing happened. It was six A.M., and I was at the church for an early prayer meeting with some of the men of the congregation.

Believe me, if receiving an insight or revelation depended upon how one feels, I would have been the last candidate in the world that day. I was not sick, but I do not exactly come out of bed whistling at five A.M. It is not my idea of beginning the day with a thrill, as that time of the morning strikes me more as being "yesterday" than "today." (Who would join me in a movement for declaring *any* day is not officially begun until after six A.M.?)

Anyway, as I knelt with the others—feeling more that I was trying to keep awake than that I was being very successful at prayer—I sensed the Holy Spirit wanting to speak to me. The words impressing my consciousness were completely baffling to me:

The four "angels at the corners" mentioned the other night are the four living creatures described in the book of Revelation, chapter four.

You could have knocked me over with a feather!

Here I am, I thought to myself, *trying to pray like an obedient disciple; and now God* (for I did, in fact, believe it was He) *drops something like this on me!* I did not know how to respond; it seemed such a peculiar thing. I was even tempted to say, "Sure, Lord, sure they are! The four cherubim . . . right!"

I did not truly feel that way, of course, but it was tempting to respond in the same way one might patronize a teasing friend. Still, I was troubled by the fact that I could not escape the conviction this was valid. *Why, entire cult systems have begun with less material than this!* I chuckled to myself.

But it was no joke. I knew the Lord was teaching me something so I opened the Bible and turned to the passage of Scripture that had been brought to my attention.

In Revelation 4, the apostle John describes his sense of being transported to the throne of God itself—into the central site of heaven, to the heaven of the heavens, so to speak. After describing the awesome splendor of the majestic radiance emanating from the throne, he describes the creatures surrounding it as all of them exult in high worship and adoration of the Creator.

Closest to the throne, in a role that apparently both protects the glory of God's seat of rule as well as directs praise unto His glory, are "four living creatures" of absolutely startling appearance (vv. 6–8). The description identifies them as part of the angelic order of the *cherubim*—a word formed from the plural of the Hebrew *keruwb,* or in English, *cherub.*

These creatures are mentioned in more than twenty passages in the Bible, with the word *cherub* or *cherubim* occurring nearly one hundred times. They are always associated with the throne of God and worship being directed to Him. In fact, before Lucifer fell and became Satan, the adversary, he was probably the leader of this order: "You were the anointed cherub who covers."[1] This probably refers to his being assigned authority to lead the worship of all heaven unto God, and to direct the choirs of glory to the praise of the Almighty. (This explains even more readily how immediately vulnerable Lucifer was to the temptation of wanting praise to be directed to himself instead, since he was so central to the throne.)

But here in Revelation, the central point of worship is focused and led by the team of four cherubim. Here, for the first time in Scripture, we actually see them at worship—and we are made witnesses to the power of their influence when they do.

> The four living creatures ... do not rest day or night, saying: "Holy, holy, holy, Lord God Almighty, who was and is and is to come!" Whenever the living creatures give glory and honor and thanks to Him who sits on the throne who lives forever and ever ... [others around the throne] fall down before Him who

> sits on the throne and worship Him who lives for-
> ever and ever, and cast their crowns before the
> throne, saying: "You are worthy, O Lord, to receive
> glory and honor and power; for You created all
> things, and by Your will they exist and were cre-
> ated."   Revelation 4:8–11

The force and flow of the cherubim at worship seem to sweep out from the throne of God to captivate and summon all others present to do the same. And as the passage concludes (which continues in chapter 5) the entire universe is caught up in praise to God.

What captured my attention as I read this again, however, was not the angelic beings themselves so much as their position around the throne. The fact that they are "around"—in close proximity to the throne—and that there are four in number did correlate with the words our youth pastor had shared those few nights before. But even now, I did not really understand anything of clear or abiding substance; and feeling very hesitant to make any point of pursuing the matter, I dropped it once again.

If I had labored farther in quest of some arcane insight or special meaning, I would probably have been dubious about my conclusions. Instead, I laid the matter to rest and, for all my concern, that is precisely where it would have stayed. That was not to be.

About two weeks afterward I had just driven into the church parking lot, had gathered my things to take into the office and was walking toward the back door of the building with my mind only on what a beautifully clear day it was, when it happened. It was as though I had walked into a room in which someone had explained a complicated idea on a chalkboard, and just as if you could grasp the whole of that explanation in one split second, I "saw" it!

When I had reflected earlier on the words spoken and the text given, I had long since satisfied myself that God was *not* saying that the four cherubim who surrounded His throne had now relocated to Van Nuys, California! Such an idea was hilariously ludicrous! But suddenly, I was imbued with the knowledge of a powerful principle that is as applicable to anyplace on earth. The only proviso is that the persons at such a place commit themselves to worshiping God as a way of life.

In that micro-second, without any computation or analysis on my part, the Holy Spirit settled the following points of understanding in my mind:

1.   Every picture of God's throne shown in the Bible describes both His glory and the presence of these angelic beings (Isaiah 6; Ezekiel 1; Revelation 4).

2.   The position of the four angelic beings is *central to* the throne—that is, in the midst, in immediate proximity, and *around* the throne—that is, at four points in circumference (Revelation 4:6).

3.   These creatures lead and stimulate praise, and seem to seek to draw all the earth into chorus with their worship of the Creator (Isaiah 6:3). As a congregation, we had set ourselves to be part of such continued praise and worship—honoring God's Word and glorifying God's Son.

4.   The Bible says God is enthroned upon those praises (Psalm 22:3), and that when His name is *hallowed* ("Holy, holy, holy Lord!"), there is a place prepared for His Kingdom's throne to "come," and for His will to be done "on earth as it is in heaven" (Matthew 6:9–10).

Thus it was, in the light of these amalgamated facts, that in a single instant the Holy Spirit helped me see a magnificent reality I would otherwise never have grasped:

Our worship as a congregation had brought this house into biblical alignment with the throne of God! That is why we experienced the presence of the angels: They did not come "here," but our worship aligned us with them "there"!

This was not a signal of any achievement on our part, but was simply the inevitable reward of worship. It is a benefit available to anyone, anyplace, who will commit himself, or themselves, to having a "house" founded in worshiping the true and living God, and exalting His Son Jesus Christ. I saw that the four angelic beings had not taken their stations at our address; rather, our worship had aligned us with God's address!

Thus, our youth pastor sensed four angels at the corners of that little building due to the fact that our worship was aligning an insignificant site on the earth level of things with the ultimately significant site—God's throne! Further, as the two conjoined—as "the Lord was enthroned amid His people's praise"—the four angelic creatures at their posts around His throne became positioned coincidentally at the four corners of our place. They had not been running from address to address where praise occurred (and I never believed they had!), but in the realm of the eternal, we had drawn near to *Him.*

Perhaps this is the heart of James' words:

But He gives more grace. Therefore He says: "God resists the proud, but gives grace to the humble." Therefore submit to God. Resist the devil and he will flee from you. *Draw near to God and He will draw near to you.* Cleanse your hands, you sinners; and purify your hearts, you double-minded.

James 4:6–8 (author's emphasis)

Jesus said, "The hour is coming, and now is, when you will not worship either at this mountain or at that mountain in Jerusalem."[2] In these words He was noting that *where* worship takes place is not the central issue anymore; rather, *that* it does. In short, He adds, "The Father is seeking people whose worship is spiritually alive and true-hearted" (John 4:24, paraphrase). Thereby, He has afforded us a certain and precious guarantee. We need never be without God's presence. He is *seeking* worshipers, so we can be assured that if we will worship Him, He will show up!

Worship invites and gives place for the glory of the Lord to be realized and to bless at a given place. It is an act of the sovereign God's choice and grace, but it is not arbitrary, random or accidental. It is a decisive action He promises in response to genuine human hunger for Him. Our participation, praise and worship, welcoming the entry of God's Kingdom presence, is not a humanistic attempt at getting God to move. But rather, as the psalmist puts it, we stand before Him invitingly with "waiting" praises.

Praise is awaiting You, O God, in Zion; and to You the vow shall be performed. O You who hear prayer, to You all flesh will come.   Psalm 65:1–2

Thus a sustained stance of worship establishes an alignment in the invisible realm, but in a real and powerful way places God's throne "in the midst" of your or my situation. Any person, or people, who wills to be a worshiper can make his "house" a center of God's visiting grace and glory.

The Key Is Worship

The absolute and constant in this process of realizing God's Kingdom presence "where you live" is worship. Worship is foundational to the entry of God's rule. The Lord's Prayer teaches it.

Look how it opens—with a divine call to worship: "When you pray, say 'Our Father in heaven, holy is Your name.' " The words are not unlike the "Holy, holy, holy" that pervades all worship around God's throne, but, curiously enough, these more familiar words of the Lord's Prayer are not usually perceived as worship; rather, simply as a reverent expression. Yet, in the Old English, *hallowed*—as used in this phrase, generally presumed only to remind us to revere God's name—is actually a declaration of commitment to begin with worship. Thus, Jesus is saying, "On the basis of the relationship I have given you with the loving Father, proceed to worship Him for His worthiness and unto His glory."

Following worship, notice how Jesus' lesson on prayer proceeds with a direct call for the entry of God's ruling presence—*here and now* in Kingdom power. Jesus instructs us to pray, "Thy Kingdom come, Thy will be done on earth as it is in heaven."

Familiar words, but what do they mean?

Perhaps you take them as I once did, presuming they were a prayer about the future—for a "someday" when Christ will come again and establish His perfect Kingdom on earth. That day is coming, of course, and it is perfectly proper that we should pray for it.[3] But Jesus' call to prayer for the Kingdom's entry is intended not simply for His future Kingdom, but also for this present era of the Church's ministry. The Greek verb form is immediate, active, imperative. In other words, the time is *now,* and the King of all is definitively to be invited: "Let it come at this point in time—here, please, Sir."

We do not need a church meeting in a home to make this happen where we live. But we do need to consecrate our houses in worship to the Lord. Moreover, it is not just our dwelling places that can be aligned with God's throne. Second Corinthians 4:7 notes the divinely intended plan that our most natural circumstances be potential dwelling places for His splendor and glory: "We have this treasure in earthen vessels, that the excellence of the power may be of God and not of us." Here is God's peerless and pristine glory, ready to be invested in finite and fallible human settings, but too few seem bold enough to accept these possibilities for their "houses," thinking such glory is far beyond their capacity of faith or ability to receive.

But listen: This is livable spirituality, far removed from the impossible pretensions exhibited by people whose definition of *spiritual* is "unreal." A false or contrived value of the meaning of spirituality tempts some people to take themselves too seriously, and not to take God seriously enough. Efforts at being holy in our own power exhaust our ability to draw on and rejoice in His holiness. Dear friend, we are talking about our houses coming into perfect alignment with the doorposts of God's Kingdom throne room. But we are not expecting—because He is not planning—that it will make our homes into spiritually spooky places.

I have always felt a little uneasy around people who make spiritual life sound too "spiritualistic." It is certainly not because I object to biblical disciplines of holiness, or to a strong belief in the supernatural works of God. It is that nothing is farther from the truth than the notion that holiness is ethereally impractical, or that a commitment to faith in God's supernatural power is synonymous with bizarre practices or weird people.

True spirituality and fuzzy mysticism are not related.

Perhaps I should assert that there is cause for some to abhor the idea of a "religious" home. By "religious" in this context, I am referring to ritualized, stiff and stodgy pietism. It is not true piety, but a brand of supposed godliness that cultivates a hard-heartedness toward the Lord and His ways. The perpetrators become heavy-handed and the child victims become embittered. Efforts at living worship deteriorate quickly into dead ritual. This malady occurs when, in saying grace over a meal, a service is held at the table while dinner chills; or when an all-knowing voice intones a Bible verse over every action.

I remember a set of books we were given when our kids were little, about a Christian family with young children. They had many excellent features, but, honestly, it seemed that no matter what happened, "Father always had a Scripture verse for it." I'm sure the writer intended to communicate something of the relevancy of Scripture to our daily life, but too often the story became contrived and I actually got tired of Daddy always having a verse.

I nearly felt like screaming: "Hey, Dad! Can't we just let life happen *once* without a text!" I certainly don't object to the integration of the Word with life's circumstances. That is what my whole life is about. But forced spiritualizing in a home setting can too easily become the means that eventually drives a wedge between Christian parents and their children. It can breed a low-grade rebellion and label parents as out-of-touch. Few children have survived that kind of packaged, pompous piety.

So when the Holy Spirit fills a life or a house, let's not expect Him to neutralize the true humanity that God the Father created. He can work in *true* "holiness"—the restoration of God's original, pre-sin-tainted plan for human beings. The Holy Spirit's investiture in human flesh will not produce a hybrid—something neither completely divine nor completely human. Instead, His presence in our lives, as in our homes, will bring about a thoroughly spiritual and genuinely natural person: people who are holy in their happiness and happy expressions of holiness. Look at Jesus! He is the evidence that holiness and humanity can be blended successfully, beautifully and without affectation.

A Healthy Home

Certain principles and practices will lead toward the development of happy, human, holy homes. Let's take an overview of them because, just as there were certain matters we examined to avoid a leprous house, so there are certain practices to apply to experience a healthy one.

1. Take Communion at home.

Since I described Anna's and my observing the Lord's Table in the face of a spiritually oppressive time, and then leading our children to do the same, you have already seen a practical application of this rite in the home. First Corinthians talks about both the power of the blood of Jesus and the power of His healing presence (because of His broken body) as aspects of promise that need to be part of the testimony in our homes. The early Church was a *home* church. That is not an argument against the desirability of enjoying church facilities today, or criticism of lovely or commodious sanctuaries. But the fact should certainly break the back of any notion that the Lord's Table is inappropriate for personal or family observance in our homes.

When Israel prepared to leave Egypt, the blood of a lamb on the doorposts spared their homes. Similarly, God is calling out families and individuals to leave the slavery of past sin and enter a miracle work of freedom in the light of His Word and His glorious presence. And it starts—as with Israel's deliverance—right in the home!

Keep the elements for the Lord's Supper available in your home: a small container of grape juice (kept refrigerated) and a box of matzos or bread set apart for this purpose. Be certain that any participation is understood so that children experience *today* what God directed long ago:

> "And it shall be, when your children say to you, 'What do you mean by this service?' that you shall say, 'It is the Passover sacrifice of the Lord, who passed over the houses of the children of Israel in Egypt when He struck the Egyptians and delivered our households.' "　　　　　Exodus 12:26–27

One young couple in our congregation explained Communion to their six-year-old this way:

- When they partake of the bread, they have her join them in saying, "Thank You, Jesus, that because Your body was broken, mine can be made whole."

- When they partake of the cup, they say together, "Thank You, Jesus, that because You bled on the cross, my sins can be forgiven."

That is a simple way of explaining the Lord's Table, but for a child of this age and level of understanding, it is enough. As children become older, more can be explained. And a short review of 1 Corinthians 11 is not a bad idea for the adults present, either!

We have never recommended such common or frequent exercise of this New Testament privilege at home that it becomes glib, religious or meaningless. Regularity is not the point as much as the beauty of the family partaking together and with understanding. Sensitivity, sobriety of mood, scripturality of participation—all these factors ought to be observed.

2. Sing at home.

I wrote these words to my congregation in one Sunday's communiqué:

> Sing in your house! See what a difference a "praise atmosphere" can make. Records and tapes are good, but don't depend on others to do all the praising for you.

"But my voice sounds miserable!"

O.K. So don't necessarily inflict it on others—but sing when alone (the practice may help!). Sing at the day's beginning and sing at the end. Sing together around the

dinner table as your occasional expression of table grace.
Let's let our houses be *filled* with the song of the Lord!

Look at the promises that describe the power of song:

Isaiah 54:1—Song creates the environment for new life
when barrenness has blocked our fruitfulness.

Psalm 32:6–7—Song works deliverance when singing
saints refuse to be quenched in spirit by threatened bondage.

2 Chronicles 20:21–22—Song declares, "The battle is
the Lord's," when trial comes; and song will scatter the
adversary's opposition.

Colossians 3:16 and Ephesians 5:18–19—Song (1)
keeps you filled with the Holy Spirit, and (2) makes God's
Word rich in practice.

Job 38:4–7—Song attends God's majestic actions of creation. Give Him an atmosphere to release His creativity
in your home and circumstance.

3. Pray at your house.

It is so obvious as to not need saying, but the very
mention of making ours "a house of prayer" can seem
beyond reach. How can a place . . .

- filled with the hubbub of kids running, playing, screaming . . .

- stressed by the tension of tough situations or even arguments . . .

- resounding with the festivities of seasonal celebrations
. . .

- echoing with the morning cries, "Hurry, or you'll be late
. . ."

- roaring with the sound of the vacuum, dishwasher and clothes dryer . . .

- crackling with the yips and yowls of the dog chasing the cat . . .

how can this place be "a house of prayer"!

Take hope. Remember, God has not called you to found a monastery, but only to give Him a place where He is welcomed. Don't feel less than a candidate for the glory that attends a house of prayer because your prayer life does not match Martin Luther's, Mother Teresa's, George Muller's or St. Francis'! Just pray. Pray when you rise. Pray as you walk through the house. Pray as you make the coffee. Pray as you shower, dress, cook.

Yes! Of course, take time to stop and be with God in private devotion, but do not feel that is all that counts.

Pray as a family. Make table prayer meaningful. Even though it is brief, it can be brightly blessed if it is kept from becoming a recitation and is made fresh as something of life is regularly spoken.

And you do not necessarily need a ritualized family altar to have a spiritual home. When it rises naturally, it is powerfully precious, for the kids enter in as genuine participants instead of feeling they have been marshaled for divine duty.

4. Testify in your house.

Lead your family to talk together about the good things God has done for each of you. Amazingly, many families allow the supernatural side of their experience to remain unexpressed. But that is the prevailing mood that creates a cleavage between the miraculous and the mundane—and it is worth resisting. Don't let the realities of your visible/daily/natural life be wedged apart from your invisible/here-and-now/spiritual life.

"Well, what did Jesus help you do today?" we often say as we start table talk at our evening dinnertime. And when we pray together, because we have sought to make the supernatural as natural in our home as breathing, we have always intermittently prayed "in the Spirit" as well as "with the understanding" (1 Corinthians 14:15). It is unsurprising, then, that our kids, now grown up, walk in the expectation of the Holy Spirit's presence with them daily. At home He was not made into a "mysterious Other" who manifested Himself only at high moments of ecstasy or once a year at youth camp. He was right there filling us in the middle of cornbread and pork 'n' beans.

5. Speak the Word in your house.

Besides your own devotional Bible reading, how about standing in the center of your living room periodically and reading a psalm aloud? Let the same Word who brought the universe into being penetrate the created materials that constitute the fabric of your dwelling. It is that same Word who presently sustains all things in the created order (Colossians 1:17), so you can expect His declaration to affect the relative order in your home. It's mighty!

When our oldest daughter, Becki, with her husband, Scott, and the kids, moved into a house that had been occupied by an unusually depressed couple, they "felt" it in the place. At first, thinking it was mere imagination, they hesitated doing what came to mind, but then decided it was the leading of the Lord. They set up an audiocassette player, and over the period of two weeks played the entire New Testament in each room!

I suppose some reader may interpret this as superstition, but that could only be because they do not know this couple. They are as typical as any young American suburbanites. Dad jogs two to three miles daily; Mom shuttles kids to school and Little League games; the kids have their normal complement of problems and joys; the family gets sick and then well again, has times of financial crunch and the victory, etc. But they have tapped the power of glory on their house. And the glory of God's Word during that time it was "sounded through each room" brought a freshness and dispelled the gloom that seemed to have been left by its former occupants.

6. Keep your house bright.

The talk, attitudes and entertainment that characterize your home either pollute or illumine the place. It is important to cultivate a genuine mood of hope in your home. Hope is not a "cross-your-fingers" kind of dreamy-eyed sentiment. *Hope is the solid conviction that God has a genuine, custom-made, blessed plan for you and your family, and that He is totally committed to seeing it fulfilled!* When that idea dominates your heart it will light your life—and your house.

We are the stewards of this brightness, however. It can be dulled, dampened or doused by tolerated moodiness, unapologized-for and unforgiven sharpness in speech, unworthy music, activities or videos.

I use the old word *douse,* meaning to strike the sails or to put out the light, because of an expression often used by my dad, a former Navy man. "Douse the glimmer," he would shout, if he saw that any of us kids had left a light on somewhere—words that would send us racing in military-like obedience. But here I have used the word with reference to the possibility of *keeping the light on—* to refuse whatever influence would extinguish the brightness of God's glory light in your home. Those home-fires are ours to have *always,* burning with the brightness of His blessing and presence.

7. Consecrate your house.

After living for twelve years in the same place just four blocks from the church, Anna, the kids and I moved to a new parsonage, a much larger house, about nine miles away. The elders and congregation provided this more spacious home for the primary reason that entertaining groups where we had lived was becoming impossible. With the growth of our congregation, even the smallest groups of key leaders would not fit in the parsonage living-dining area.

Because we have always loved to entertain—Anna is *so* creative, and is a just-plain-devoted worker— hospitality has always been a hallmark of our home. And so we moved one week in mid-November, and started to settle in over the next several days.

It was not until two weeks later that I was reminded of something I had intended to do when we moved in. I had intended to *establish the boundaries* in prayer, but had put it off, being so busy with the move, settling in and general daily duties. By that phrase, I mean I was intent on applying two verses of God's Word to our new living site:

1. Words spoken to Abraham: "Arise, walk in the land through its length and its width, for I give it to you" (Genesis 13:17).

2. Words spoken to Joshua: "Now therefore, arise. . . .

Every place that the sole of your foot will tread upon I have given you" (Joshua 1:2–3).

Being thoroughly convinced that God's principles are timeless and His promises fully applicable to us today, I wanted to declare "our possession" of this new house. We had moved in by every physical measure; now I wanted to affirm our taking *spiritual* dominion.

Two things are parallel in these words of promise God spoke to these heroes of historic, powerful and practical faith: (1) God said, "I've given this to you," and (2) He directed each of them to possess it by actually identifying with it "foot by foot."

So before dawn one morning just after Thanksgiving, I rose and dressed warmly against the autumn chill. The early light edging up from the east heralded the sun's progress toward a new day. It was clear, brisk and frosty.

I was excited. I sensed the joy of knowing I was applying God's promises and the power of His pledged presence to our new place of residence. I began by walking across the front line of our property, along the street, wanting to be through with that area before people were up and about in the neighborhood. I was just turning west at the north corner of our lot when I felt impressed to stop. I stood there, waiting pensively on the Lord, when the impression became clear: *Raise four pillars.*

It might have been my own thoughts, desiring to consecrate the property to God, or it might have been the Holy Spirit. But it really makes little difference, because the practicality, the biblical nature of it and the beauty inherent in the idea all converge to make it as spiritually vital as anything God's Spirit would approve. I knew what to do and how to do it.

Standing at the northeast corner of our new homesite, I lifted my hands and began to praise the Lord. As I did I declared to God the establishment of an invisible pillar at that site. With praise and in faith I set myself to do the same at each corner, committing them into alignment with God's throne and establishing barricades against all dark powers. I expressed my thanks for His goodness in allowing us this place and declared: "Through the doorposts of these pillars I invite You to come and dwell in Kingdom glory in our home and upon our family. I name the pillar Praise."

Pacing slowly down the northern boundary of our lot I came to the northwest corner. "Rejoice!" The word resounded in my soul, and I quietly began to sing and clap my hands in happiness for the promises of God's blessing on all who walk in His ways. You may not approve of what may appear to be unusual gullibility, but I leave you with this fact: Even while I was singing and clapping, a bird flew into a tree above me and began to chirp *in perfect cadence to my song's tempo!* Take it or leave it: I felt the Creator had prompted one of His creatures to join in this moment with affirmation of my actions.

I have never told anyone other than our own family what I named the other pillars as I proceeded around the boundaries and "raised" each of the four with praise. I think people should ask the Lord to show them appropriate names if they raise pillars. There is no formula for setting the doorposts of His Kingdom at your home, for I believe He wants it to be characteristic of your life, to be custom-made to your own relationship with Him. I do propose this practice, however:

Consecrate your dwelling to the Lord. Make a definitive act of presenting the physical site to Him. Whether it is an apartment on the twelfth floor of a 25-story building, a mansion in Newport, a condo in Minneapolis, a mobile home in Phoenix, a crowded little two-bedrooms-for-us-and-the-kids house in Portland, or . . . describe your place.

Present it to the Lord. Pace around its dimensions and raise your own pillars of promise. And as you do, there is strong reason to believe He will walk right between those doorposts of His Kingdom and dwell at your house.

He always comes to abide where people align their hearts with His throne.

Notes

[1] Ezekiel 28:14.

[2] John 4:21 (author's paraphrase).

[3] Prayers for the ultimate visitation of the Kingdom, when Christ comes to earth again, are in the words the apostle John uses to conclude the canon of Scripture: "Even so, come, Lord Jesus!" (Revelation 22:20). Or Paul's *Maranatha!* may spring forth from our lips in anticipation as well: "The Lord is coming!"

6

Houses of the Kingdom

I was driving north on the Hollywood Freeway, paralleling the swatch of trees that border the highway as it cuts through Chandler Park. The four miles to the Sherman Way turnoff were being swallowed rapidly as I glided along with the early afternoon traffic.

Ten months had passed since our arrival at the church in Van Nuys. We had come only to fulfill a request to take an interim assignment and, consequently, had no great expectations for the short transition term we were to fill. But a few weeks before the freeway "moment" that was about to happen, I had received a strong sense of direction from the Holy Spirit that we were to stay at this small pastorate.

It was not a direction accepted without a struggle.

Better opportunities seemed to beckon, but I had felt trapped by God. I could not escape the inner call to lay down any human ambitions or personal presuppositions about my future. Then in a life-changing encounter just a few days before, I had surrendered to my sense of God's purpose and will. And now I felt peace.

Still, for all this, rather than feeling expectancy or sweeping vision about my assigned place of duty, I felt only a peaceful sense of obedience. I presumed I was now destined simply to labor faithfully in a small pastorate. I was not disappointed, and I felt no sense of rejection by the Lord for being consigned by Him to so unimpressive a place. In fact, I felt a surprising and comforting contentment to be in His will and know it. My mindset was on anything but "great expectations." God was about to burst that bubble of what some would suppose is the requirement for humility.

Without any anticipation on my part, as I was cruising forward with the flow of the freeway, words seemed suddenly to distill from out of "nowhere," landing on my awareness: *You mustn't think too small.*

At the time I was not thinking of my future, the church—anything like that. I was simply driving on an L.A. freeway—that's all that was on my mind! But now, I was jarred to full alert. Instantly and intuitively— without reflection—I knew that it was the Lord, and that He was addressing those feelings I held about being placed in a tiny, obscure pastorate. I was stunned. Then He spoke again: *You mustn't think too small, or you will get in My way.*

I have never been criticized for small thinking. It is not characteristic of me. But in the breaking process of God's dealing with my heart over the preceding weeks, I had become convinced that that humbling meant my whole future would be relatively obscure.

This resignation to anonymity had not made me unhappy, nor did I feel pitiful. But something of human aspiration *had* been broken, and now God wanted to instill *His* expectations in its place. Here He was, calling, insisting that I allow my heart and mind to be stretched to receive something more than I had supposed.

The voice spoke again, once more repeating the first words, then adding to them: *You mustn't think too small, or you will get in My way; for I have set Myself to do a great work.*

With these words, a vision flashed into my mind—a scene snatched from the future, barely perceived, but sufficient to convince me that the largeness of the work would involve both property and buildings as well as people. It was *not* my vision, just as those were not my words. I knew the difference. I continued on in the flow of traffic as I had before, but now everything was different. God had let me know that He was committed to doing something beyond my imagination.

In the years since, as my brief tenure at The Church On The Way developed into permanency, I have seen this as a principle: God seeks to increase His work *in* each of us so that He might release His life *through* each of us—through our homes, our families, our business dealings and under our whole aegis of influence. He is committed to making us people of promise and purpose in every area of our lives! It requires, however, more than a dream or vision.

Preparatory to a visitation of God's glory on our houses is the need for *reshaping* our thinking. This is at the heart of Jesus' announcement to "repent, for the Kingdom of God is at hand!" Nothing short of *renewing* our souls, *reteaching* our ideas and a *refilling* of His Spirit will equip us for glory.

As a result of watching Him bring about His workings, I have discovered a combination of truths that seem essential to the fullest release of His glory/grace in an individual or group. For me, understanding took place in the context of my life—my profession—and so I relate it in "church-life" terms. But within my description are principles applicable to all professions from attorneys to housewives, from students to gas station managers, from clerks to physicians. These three principles are for anyone and everyone:

1.   Extending the love of God to others is not a zealous program but a natural, comfortable lifestyle.

2.   This lifestyle opens most clearly when the meaning of the Kingdom is understood.

3.   The fruit of this lifestyle abounds only when a person opens to and lives in the fullness of the Holy Spirit.

These dynamic points not only converged in my own understanding, but affected drastically my approach to serving Jesus as His disciple. Then, as I began to teach these points, I found even the most ordinary people beginning to view themselves in a new way as it became conceivable that God would fill all their "house," flowing Jesus' life and health into and through them! Let's look at each of them.

1. Extending God's Love . . . Naturally

As I began to let God reshape my thinking about extending His glory, my approach to evangelism changed. I became no less concerned about the unsaved, but I began to discern between human and holy methods of reaching them in my own public or private encounters. Until this

I had viewed public church services as the essential setting to persuade the lost to decide for Christ. Further, I had felt that any conversations I had with an unbeliever ought ideally to be geared pointedly for witnessing, meaning doing anything possible to jockey the conversation toward a place in which I could use a "plan."

Raised in this mindset, I saw my pastoral task as essentially twofold: (1) preach the Gospel; and (2) teach others how to witness. Both involved proven methods for sharing the gospel of God's love. Evangelistic sermons with moving altar calls were the public means; training members in planned conversations usable for personal evangelistic encounters was the private means.

Let me pause to interject here that I carry no brief against any approach to evangelism. These words above are not intended as critical or demeaning to whatever approach anyone feels moved to employ. But I was discovering a *spirit*—a mood and mindset that would extend the concept of evangelism beyond these limits. It began to manifest in each person who perceived himself or herself more naturally as Christ's official representative. The amazing thing was how satisfying and unguiltdriven life became by learning simply to live, love and serve Jesus in His power and authority, doing whatever or ministering to whomever the Comforter (the Holy Spirit) brought *comfortably* into our lives.

At this time I had had years of experience in training people about plans for personal evangelism. I had also found that those efforts usually tended to produce more guilt than effectiveness. Now, while still not opposing those methods, I was instead seeking a way to nurture those I taught in a *concept,* instead of simply training them in a *method.* I was beginning to see how people who embrace a concept—an idea or a point of understanding—can more easily and naturally apply it to any situation in life. Those who know only a plan must manipulate encounters to make room for their message. The Holy Spirit seemed to have a more workable way for more people—a way to extend all of God's love with all of the Holy Spirit's resources.

The basis of the concept was the fact that Jesus did not simply commission us to go and tell people how to get saved. His commission was broader:

"Speak the Gospel to the poor . . . speak liberty to captive souls.
Heal sick bodies . . . bind up broken hearts.
Visit the afflicted, imprisoned and bedridden.
Offer cooling water to thirsty lips and restore sight to the blind.
Confront and usurp the control of entrenched demon powers."[1]

The essence of His approach was to shape His disciples with spiritual readiness so that they might love people in the middle of their need. He taught them to be confident when praying for the hurting, and to be sensitive when reaching out to those who showed a human hunger for the love God was ready to give *through them*. He was preparing Kingdom people—people who understand who they are, what the Church is to be and how they can be exactly that. These are people who move into each day as common, everyday people, but who become naturally supernatural—that is, available to the Holy Spirit's direction and enablement. With this view of evangelism in focus, I came to the second dynamic principle in understanding the Kingdom.

2. The Gospel Jesus Taught

It was my looking at the Gospel the way Jesus taught it that began helping the people I served. This was the key to their becoming infused with a genuine sense of their potential for *extraordinary effectiveness as ordinary people*. Let me elaborate.

The essential heartbeat of the Gospel Jesus preached is found in His words *the Kingdom of God*. I had been blind earlier to the awesome, refreshing truth inherent in this, His message. But while teaching the synoptic Gospels, something happened: I became imbued with the richness of His ministry and our possibilities as agents of His Kingdom. My assignment to teach Matthew, Mark and Luke at a college-seminary level had brought me into confrontation with the fact that all my life I had spoken of a Kingdom—indeed, been born into it—but still had not understood that Kingdom's definition, dimensions and full dynamic. I wondered, having been "so close and yet so far," how many other Christians have a similar lack of understanding of this conceptual keystone to the life of the living Church.

Even though the phrase *Kingdom of God*[2] occurs more than one hundred times in the Gospels and is the heart of Jesus' message, I was amazed that I had never had it clearly defined to me. For myself, and most Christians I have met, *the Kingdom* was a vague, generic term seemingly used to describe anything or everything that was in any way "spiritual." In fact, common practices contributing to my fogginess on the subject were born of churchy habits of speech:

- Offerings were received "to help the work of the Kingdom of God," seeming to equate "the Kingdom" with the church as an institution.

- In evangelistic appeals, this verse is commonly quoted, "Unless one is born again, he cannot see the kingdom of God,"[3] seeming to make the Kingdom equivalent to heaven. The assumption is that the issue in this text is one's eternal destination rather than coming to know the temporal dynamic of God's Spirit now, plus eternal life forever!

- When people enter a Bible college or seminary to train for church leadership, they are described as "committing to serve a vocation in the Kingdom of God." Kingdom again seems to equal Church.

In short, *the Kingdom* was generally described either as ethereal or ecclesiastical.

But I began to see how these ideas not only missed the point of Jesus' teaching, but missed the mark of giving His followers a means to see themselves as His authorized agents. Jesus equipped His disciples to touch their "house"—that is, their *whole* world. That they did is a matter of thrilling record in Acts, and I believe the same will happen as we understand the Kingdom of God more clearly than we usually have.

Let me share in abbreviated form an outline of the concept of the Kingdom as we began to perceive and teach it.

Kingdom Rule

The Bible makes two things clear about God's rule throughout the universe:

First, He is almighty. No power transcends His (Psalm 19:1–6).

Second, He delegates His rule of planet earth to man (Genesis 1:26–28). "The heaven, even the heavens, are the Lord's; but the earth He has given to the children of men" (Psalm 115:16).

Kingdom Lost

A double disaster occurred when mankind fell from the place of relationship with God and rulership under Him. When he submitted to Satan's lies, man lost both—his place in relationship *with* God and his rule of this earth *under* God. Not only this, but in obeying the adversary, man lost the authority God had given him over the earth. It was forfeited into the hands of the devil.

Kingdom Usurped

Since that time, the rule of the world has been in the grip of Satan, who is called alternately "the god of this world" (2 Corinthians 4:4, KJV) and "the ruler of this world" (John 14:30). We are told specifically that "the whole world lies in the power of the evil one," in the same sense that Paul speaks of "this present evil age" (1 John 5:19, NASB; Galatians 1:4).

Kingdom Ruined

What God created and called "good" has not changed fundamentally, but it has all come under a wicked, rebellious rulership. The devil both rules and multiplies his destructiveness upon mankind, and generally escapes blame. Ironically, most of what people attribute to "acts of God"—heartache, disaster, war, strife, bloodshed, broken lives, broken homes, diseased bodies, suffering and finally death—are *not* God's actions or His will. Instead, they are the direct and combined result of man's lost rule through disobedience and Satan's takeover rule with his program of ruin and destruction.

Kingdom Come

Jesus, the Messiah, the Son of God, came as both Savior and King. His mission was twofold. First, as the "second Adam" He came to rescue mankind and through His death to restore our relationship with the living God. Second, as resurrected Lord He has risen to begin the reinstatement of mankind to his intended estate as a "ruler-in-life" under God (Romans 5:12).

Jesus' ministry demonstrated what happens when God's rule reenters the human scene: "Repent, for the Kingdom of God is here with you now." He summoned people to repentance and forgiveness, while He also showed them evidence of the transforming and transcendent power of the Kingdom. He did that by restoring fallen humans through love, grace and forgiveness, and by casting out the dominating darkness of demonic, hellish works through His mighty miracles and healings. Both orders of action confirmed that God's rule was reentering this present world. Whenever people received His rule by acknowledging Jesus as Messiah, the Holy Spirit's anointing on Him confirmed the word of the Gospel of the Kingdom. The Kingdom is being manifest because the King was here (Acts 2:22; Luke 24:19; John 3:33–35; 5:19).

Kingdom Victory

Throughout His ministry, Jesus trained others to do the same things He did. He told them He would die and rise again, and then be taken from them (Matthew 20:18–

19; John 14:19–21). It was not until after His resurrection that the reality of it all gripped His disciples' hearts. It was then they truly began to see how His death, resurrection and ascension to follow had secured man's restoration to the Father, conquered death and the spell its fear binds upon mankind. They were beginning to see how Jesus had broken Satan's death grip on the planet. A new order was opening. They soon expected that whenever this news was proclaimed, it would be attended in its spread with holy power—spiritual power!

Kingdom Promise

To make that power available to all of His people, Jesus promised that the Holy Spirit would come and enable the spread of the Kingdom. The Holy Spirit would work through Jesus' disciples in just the same way He had worked through Jesus. Jesus said:

> "Most assuredly, I say to you, he who believes in Me, the works that I do he will do also; and greater works than these he will do, because I go to My Father. And whatever you ask in My name, that I will do, that the Father may be glorified in the Son. If you ask anything in My name, I will do it. If you love Me, keep My commandments. And I will pray the Father, and He will give you another Helper, that He may abide with you forever, even the Spirit of truth, whom the world cannot receive, because it neither sees Him nor knows Him; but you know Him, for He dwells with you and will be in you."
> John 14:12–17

Thus, He began to deepen their understanding of what He meant when He taught them, "I will build My church." He had said that the powers of hell itself would not be able to prevail against them, "and I will give you the keys of the kingdom of heaven" (Matthew 16:18–19). Here was the explanation: Their dynamic for being His authorized agents with Kingdom authority would come through the presence and power of the Holy Spirit (Acts 1:4–8; Luke 24:49).

Kingdom Power

The advent of the Holy Spirit at Pentecost launched the Church. He anointed every member with the King's anointing, ensuring that His Kingdom would travel *in* them, giving them ability to deal with situations they would encounter in daily living. The Church is thus to comprise people who have been (1) *born* of the same Spirit who begot Jesus; and (2) *empowered* by the same Spirit who empowered Him. *Born of* and *baptized with* the Spirit, the Church is assigned to do business—to operate in all her "house" with all God's gracious power until the King returns again (Luke 19:13)! This gloriously balanced viewpoint keeps the proper tension between His Kingdom "come" and His Kingdom "coming." The ultimate glory of His eternal Kingdom waits until the day it is enforced upon earth at His return in final power and glory. But in the meantime His Body, the Church, is fully qualified to manifest the temporal fullness of His Kingdom's life, love and power. This will be extended by the work of the Holy Spirit where we, His Kingdom agents, are alert and available to reach with it.

Kingdom Authority

The grounds for any exercise of His Kingdom authority and dominion, the absolute and sole basis for all

Kingdom ministry, is the cross of Jesus Christ. When Jesus said He has received "all authority in heaven and on earth" (Matthew 28:18), it was following, and declared as a result of, His conquest of sin, death and hell through Calvary. His blood and His cross vanquished their power, and His resurrection fully verified His Kingship. In His cross He disarmed all hell's principalities and powers, making a public spectacle of them, triumphing over them in it (Colossians 2:15). Now, as Jesus is ascended to the right hand of the Father, with "all things under His feet" (Ephesians 1:22), the goal of His ministry is releasing yours and mine! That is why Paul prayed for believers like us,

> That you may know the exceeding greatness of God's power toward us who believe. It is that mightiness which He worked in Christ when He raised Him from the dead, and set Him at His own right hand in the heavenlies. There He reigns, far above all principality and power and might and dominion and every name, not only in this world, but also in the one to come.
>
> Ephesians 1:19–21 (author's paraphrase)

Kingdom Ministry

Here, then, is the present objective of God's Kingdom. Since the cross established the grounds of our authority; since Christ is now dwelling in His people through the Holy Spirit who is filling us; and since His resurrection displayed His mastery over the worst things hell can do; Jesus seeks now to extend His Kingdom through us (His Body) by means of the Holy Spirit in all our house.

Kingdom People

Jesus has left none of us on earth at the mercy of circumstances or the powers of hell. As members of His Body, the Church is filled with Jesus Himself. We are equipped to introduce His life, His love and His power in each situation the Holy Spirit provides for us. We have not been left on the defensive or called to preserve the status quo, but equipped to let Jesus happen through us. This brings the enjoyment of a happy partnership in His ongoing victory as His glory flows through us, touching people and circumstances with His life, until He comes back for us.

Kingdom Warfare

Kingdom triumph does not preclude the experience of warfare. Trial, weariness, temptation, affliction, attack and depression are frequent experiences of the faithful (Acts 14:21–22). True Kingdom teaching is unafraid to acknowledge the fact that, at times, difficulty or even apparent defeat affect the true believer.

Losing a skirmish or enduring extended conflict, however, are only part of the pathway toward a new dimension of conquest. "And they overcame him [the devil] by the blood of the Lamb and by the word of their testimony, and they did not love their lives to the death" (Revelation 12:11). Advance and triumph are ours to claim, but never without a struggle, and seldom without temporary casualties or apparent loss.

3. The Fullness of the Holy Spirit

As agents of His Kingdom, how—or by what continuum of power and ability—could ordinary people enter this kind of living? Kingdom insight, coupled with a simpler view of how evangelism was to be carried out, opened the way to the answer. I needed to teach our people the biblical basis for receiving the fullness of the Holy Spirit, and to lead them into that experience.

So it was that I began graciously to urge every believer to seek Christ openheartedly for the baptism with (or infilling of) the Holy Spirit.

Though sometimes debated in sectors of the Church at large, resistance to a second work of grace is diminishing all the time. The preponderance of Christians everywhere are refusing to deny the need for being filled with the Holy Spirit (both initially and ongoingly) after receiving Christ. It is becoming a global point of acknowledgment among all Christians, charismatic or not, that wherever people embrace the baptism with the Holy Spirit as a second work, the fruit of abounding New Testament Church life flourishes. The terminology and expectations of what may accompany such an experience do differ, but the importance of such a quest is perceived as essential and is pursued.

And so it is with us at The Church On The Way.

We settle for nothing less.

We hold that everyone in Christ's Body needs to be led to hunger for, seek and receive this infilling—not as a legalistic demand, but because of Jesus' command: "Receive the Holy Spirit" (John 20:22). Peter's sermon at the birth of the Church makes it perfectly clear: God's will is our receiving the same fullness of the Holy Spirit as at Pentecost. It is for *everyone, everywhere* in *every generation.*

"Repent, and let every one of you be baptized in
the name of Jesus Christ for the remission of sins;

and you shall receive the gift of the Holy Spirit. For the promise is to you and to your children [*everyone!*], and to all who are afar off [*everywhere!*], as many as the Lord our God will call [*in every generation!*]."[4]   Acts 2:38–39

As to the frequent question of whether or not today's believer should expect the same evidences of Spirit-filled life as reported in the New Testament, we have chosen not to argue but simply to accept the expectation of the supernatural. In the earliest seasons of the Church's life that the book of Acts reports, verbal and visible signs of the Holy Spirit's infilling were present. The gifts of the Spirit surrounded them; the fruit of the Spirit abounded in them. Choices like "The fruit or the gifts—which first?" or "Which gifts are most important?" were not forced then. So we take the same course, encouraging *expectancy* and discouraging *selectivity* ("Oh, I'd never want that gift!" or "I'd much rather have the fruit of the Spirit than His gifts!").

It is a joyous thing to behold the fruit of the Spirit in a person's life—the character of Christ, revealing everything from love through self-control (see Galatians 5:22–23). At the same time, how delightful to see the same person increasing in the gifts of the Spirit—the *charismata* of Christ, manifesting (as the Spirit wills) everything from a word of wisdom to an interpretation of tongues (see 1 Corinthians 12:8–9).

With specific reference to the common question today (which was never asked in the early Church), "What about speaking with tongues?," we can only admit that we normally experience that grace. We have found that when people grow in a climate that centers on (1) worshiping and glorifying Jesus; (2) living with the Word of God as our foundation for faith; and (3) walking and encouraging one another in an atmosphere of loving acceptance, it seems they just *do*—they experience the exercise of a spiritual language in their private, devotional lives. We do not pressure a superficial experience, though we clearly encourage expectancy. Still, we never disapprove of or demean any who may not as yet have spoken in tongues. Rather, we maintain an atmosphere of trust and fearlessness, knowing that the Lord Jesus will not make a fool or a fanatic of anyone who seeks *Him*.

God is seeking childlikeness in everyone; and there is something about the dependence of thirsting after righteousness and the simplicity of submitting to the Holy Spirit's supernatural work that humbles us all like children. Jesus is specifically called both the Lamb of God who takes away our sins and the Baptizer with the Holy Spirit who imbues us with power (John 1:29, 33; Luke 24:49; Acts 1:5–8), so *He*—not signs or gifts—is the central focus.

He is the One to whom we lead people to ask for Holy Spirit fullness.

We always make Christ Himself central. He's the Baptizer who will fill all who come to Him, for He said, "Blessed are those who hunger and thirst for righteousness, for they shall be filled" (Matthew 5:6). It was Jesus who also affirmed our heavenly Father's willingness in this matter: "If you then, being evil, know how to give good gifts to your children, how much more will your heavenly Father give the Holy Spirit to those who ask Him?" (Luke 11:13). It is a beautiful thing to see how the Godhead—Father, Son and Holy Spirit—merge their workings to make this a vital and fulfilling experience for those who with simplicity will ask obediently and receive this fullness openly.

Because this approach is valid, it verifies itself—not because of a doctrine but because of humble devotion to seek Jesus Christ, love His whole Church and welcome His dynamic works that we may reach and serve the world for which He died.

There is no experience in the Holy Spirit that guarantees that recipients will minister exactly as Jesus would in any given situation. Though the potential might be present, an individual's personal response might be slow. Yet we are still more committed to building people who will learn to *respond* to situations in which they can share Jesus than we are in cultivating people who try to *create* situations.

The healing of the man at the Beautiful Gate (Acts 3), for example, was a response to that cripple's request for an alms gift. Peter and John did not get together beforehand with an overwrought idea about "ministering healing to that man we've seen sitting there so many years." They were simply available for a "moment" that the Holy Spirit directed.

As another example, the revival in Samaria (Acts 8) actually occurred because Philip was driven there while fleeing persecution in Jerusalem. His response to the doors the Holy Spirit opened resulted in the city's being shaken. His method of *responding* rather than *creating opportunity* hardly seems to represent a carefully planned evangelistic crusade.

These examples are not intended as a case against planned evangelism programs or crusades. They are, however, an invitation to us all to note that at least as much "just happened" through New Testament Christians who were available to the Holy Spirit as ever happened on purpose. And yet even those things did not actually "just happen." They reveal unperceived yet purposeful and relentless design by which the Holy Spirit glorifies Christ through His Church. He finds people who understand their places in the Kingdom and He empowers and directs them there—often leading them in ways they do not perceive until afterward.

Becoming Naturally Supernatural

People of the Kingdom—*filled and ready*—need not be pretentious. Few things are more counterproductive to a naturally supernatural life than becoming preoccupied with an overriding concern to seem spiritual. Superficial piety is disturbing—not so much for the embarrassment it produces in the people who encounter it, but because of the insecurity, insensitivity and poor sense of identity it betrays in those who demonstrate it.

Jesus possessed balance.

- He was the ultimate saint, but He mixed with notorious sinners.

- He was at times the most sensitive respondent, while at other times He was the boldest initiator.

- Once He shouted aloud in the Temple courtyard; later He knelt silently at the same place to write with His finger in the dust.

Jesus was everything of humanity and nothing of superficiality; everything of godliness and nothing of religiosity. Jesus ministered the joy, life, love and health—

the glory—of His Kingdom, and He did it in the most practical, tasteful ways. And please remember: This call to such a godly naturalness, to human sensitivity in delivering Kingdom life, is not to pretend a casual or passive attitude about the lost condition of those we need to reach. But pushiness or desperation or artificiality or pompousness—none of these contrivances is essential to accomplishing the spread of the Kingdom.

What shall we do?

I recommend we cultivate people of Kingdom life and power, who will seek to live availably—available to the Holy Spirit's time and setting, who will be ever ready to extend the ministry that Holy Spirit circumstance affords and that flows naturally from a sensed debt of love to God and to man. Through such availability to Him, believers may live responsibly as Kingdom *people* living in Kingdom *power* and headed for the King's *place*. Believers are not dependent upon a feeling, or expected to push open doors. Instead they simply work daily with a sensitive heart open to the promptings of the Spirit of God. Such promptings come during the natural social interactions of day-to-day life. Their witness will flow naturally and credibly because they display a blend of sensible humanness and spiritual dynamic.

These are the new breed—the new order of priests and kings Jesus is raising to meet a world dominated by carnal and demonic machinations.

He has filled them with His life-giving Spirit.

He has taught them with the wisdom of His Word and commissioned them.

"Go. Heal the sick, cleanse the lepers, raise the dead, cast out demons. Freely you have received, freely give" (Matthew 10:8).

The New Breed

There's a brightness on their countenance,
A power in their hands:
With a sure word of authority they speak.
With the scholar they're conversant,
Understanding with a child;
Apt at warfare—or to turn the other cheek.

For this special breed of person
Has a precious freedom found;
From conformity's ice-prison they have thawed.
And in liberty they function,
Like a troop from worlds unknown.
They have come—the thrice-anointed sons of God.

Purged by water, blood and fire;
By the Word and through the cross,
Then baptized in Pentecostal tongues of flame:
They have struck the crucial balance—
Heed the law and live by grace.
They have learned the conq'ring power of Jesus' name.

So behold, world: your deliv'rers.
And behold, hell: here your fate.
You can recognize them by the glory shown
In their faces—light they captured
In the face of Christ the Lord.
He's their Captain—they His mast'ry gladly own.

Yes, there's brightness on their countenance,
There's power in their hands:
And they valiantly shatter evil's sway;
Tread on scorpions and serpents,
Heal the sick and raise the dead.
They're the radiant legions bringing God's new day.

—J.W.H.

Notes

[1] Luke 4:18–19; Mark 16:15–20; Matthew 25:34–40 (author's paraphrase).

[2] Matthew notes a frequent synonym, *Kingdom of heaven;* see Matthew 19:23–24 *et. al.* to verify Jesus' interchangeable usage.

[3] John 3:3.

[4] This book presumes the reader has already begun his life in Jesus Christ (John 3:3). Faith in the Savior begins when we (a) ask God to forgive our sins (1 John 1:9); (b) believe in His Son, Jesus, as Savior (John 1:12); (c) confess that His cross is the sole means of our salvation (Acts 4:12); and (d) declare by commitment to water baptism that He is the resurrected Lord of all (Romans 10:9–10). If you have never done this and would like assistance, it would be our pleasure to help you wherever you live. Call us at The Church On The Way, Van Nuys, California, (818) 373–8000.

7

When Strong Winds Blow

It was four A.M.

The lighted digital dial on the bedside clock was more than a time indicator: It seemed to beckon me personally. I knew I had been awakened to get up and pray.

Perhaps you have had similar experiences, for it never ceases to amaze me the way the Lord can communicate with us as His own kids. Knowing I was called to an "appointment," I slipped silently out of bed so I wouldn't bother Anna and, picking up my robe from the chair at our bedside, walked softly down the hallway, sliding my arms into the sleeves and cinching the belt around my waist. It was even then, as I padded toward the living room, that a phrase was whispered to my soul.

The tabernacle is falling.

It came as a directive, answering my prayerful inquiry as to why I was being called to prayer.

You understand the feeling—the experience; how it is that the communication of just one sentence or phrase can mean volumes. In a personal relationship, a gesture, not to mention one or two words, can indicate a bevy of things. A single sentence spoken to you by someone who knows you well can mean paragraphs, and such was my experience that morning when the Lord gave me a phrase that suddenly ignited a field of understanding for me.

I understood immediately that the Lord directed me to pray for a cluster of sticky situations. The key to my understanding was my familiarity with the portion of His Word from which He had quoted. As soon as *The tabernacle is falling* was spoken, my mind flashed to the words of the prophet Amos:

> "On that day I will raise up the tabernacle of David, which has fallen down, and repair its damages; I will raise up its ruins, and rebuild it as in the days of old."[1]

My familiarity with this passage until now, however, had not focused on fallenness so much as upon God's promise to restore, so even then I sensed He was not threatening a destruction but was promising a restoration.

The sticky situations I refer to were not imminently destructive problems anyway. Still, I recognized that the Lord was pressing my attention to present events—things in our family that, if left unattended by prayer and careful seeking of His counsel, could become serious problems.

There seemed to be a plethora of the nitty-gritty—all kinds of "stuff" congealing into the not-so-nice. Little things seemed to be happening continuously—minor points of confusion, unusual amounts of wasted time, frustration escalating into flights of temper. Furthermore, different members of the family were having recurrent bouts with minor ailments and sicknesses—all of us right down to some of our grandkids.

Besides this, I was also experiencing sporadic moments of depression. If they had been longer in duration, or if it were an ongoing problem, I would have done something about it. I would have invited elders to anoint and pray for me. I might have reviewed my diet or made sure I was sleeping enough. Sometimes there are physical explanations for why depression takes over. But in my case, these moments would come like clouds blown by a high wind, blocking the sun for only a few minutes. There was no apparent natural reason for it. A wave of depression would come. I would feel an acute sense of aloneness or helplessness. Then it would pass. But I realized that such "moments" could become a bout with despair if they stuck around.

And while there was not anything of strife in Anna's and my relationship, I was forced to admit a need. The honesty of this encounter with God alerted me to "a something else" that seemed to be going on in the house—something I could not pin down but that was there nonetheless. In retrospect, I called it an "absence of one accord." We certainly were not at each other's throats, but we seemed "out of sync" with each other. Hectic and sometimes conflicting schedules stampeded us in different directions of daily duty. A season of high intensity and compounded responsibilities for us both were not so much driving us apart as they were preventing our togetherness. Valued times of intimate conversation beside the fireplace during late evening hours had not happened for weeks.

But now the signal flag had been raised in heaven: *The tabernacle is falling*. I recognized that God was shaking me awake in more ways than getting me out of bed. My "house" was tossed and blown by winds of circumstance, and like a tent in high winds something drastic was needed to secure it.

A Billowing Tent

I am amazed at our remarkable capacity to tolerate an accumulation of this kind of domestic "garbage" without recognizing something larger behind it all. When these kinds of things happen, we can miss seeing the pattern. We become consumed with our efforts to juggle the increasing number of minor problems and, if unwarned as I was, we accumulate the problems until we can juggle no more, then—*Crash!* I had not seen the pattern in those things until that morning, but the words *The tabernacle is falling* brought a sudden perspective. I made the association between the "accumulated nitty–gritty" and the words warning of an impending collapse. Suddenly I was alert not only to these points of understanding, but also to what I had to do, and a mental picture appeared that helped me respond with prayerful sensitivity and practical wisdom.

I had been sitting in our living room now for several minutes. My family was still asleep, and I had begun to commune quietly with the Lord, hoping not to disturb anyone at this early hour. As I did, it seemed as though a video began playing across the screen of my mind.

I saw a giant tent, not unlike the old-fashioned big-tops used for the circus. The only difference was that this tent was not colored flamboyantly, but was a plain, neutral shade. Supporting it were two towering poles, constituting its primary upward thrust. (I sensed instantly that these represented Anna and me), and within the broad area covered by the giant spread of canvas were unidentifiable people and objects that I knew represented the "stuff" I had perceived by now as needing pointed prayer.

But the most notable feature of the vision was the fact that the ropes tying the tent down—strung from the bottom sides of the canvas to stakes surrounding the mobile structure—were either loosened or slack. Worse yet, the four primary ropes—larger ones placed at each corner of the tent—were completely loose and flapping violently in the wind.

As I studied the scene, it was clear that the sweep of the gale sought to come under and into the tent, rising upward like a geyser of air, bent on tearing the tent from its supports and exposing everything within it to the ripping blast of the storm.

I was moved to action—first in prayer and later in physical action that I will describe in a moment. But first, here is what I understood because of what I had seen in this vision:

- Anna's and my "house" was under pressure. Just as tornadoes are the product of two radically different weather fronts at drastically different temperatures, the peace of our house was threatened by a hostile force that we were encountering. As I said, we were not at odds, but neither were we unified in identifying and resisting the force set against us.

- The tent (tabernacle) was en route to a collapse; that is, the people and things constituting our arena of responsibility—which we "covered" through our prayer and agreement—were vulnerable to *exposure*. Should the wind whip away the tent, the two poles would still be standing in close proximity—that is, our marriage was not in danger. But we had children, grandchildren, other family, a congregation, a ministry—all involving people and circumstances that our prayers were responsible to "cover." We needed to be certain that this covering was secured by our prayer over these matters.

• The four larger ropes snapping in the wind, pulled by the wind's pressure on the tent and now tossed like threads, represented four distinct areas of duty we needed to address prayerfully—*now*. It was clear in the vision and clear in my soul—"The tabernacle is falling . . . unless you pray right now!"

The Priestly Place of Prayer

God had awakened me to remind me of the priestly place of prayer. Just as the Levites were charged with the task of raising and maintaining the Tabernacle of Moses,[2] and just as Isaiah prophesied concerning stakes and ropes,[3] I was being signaled to "wait on the Lord"—to serve the priestly role of a prayerful intercessor by strengthening the stakes and lashing the cords to them in order to secure our tabernacle.

In the Old Testament, the priests (the Levites) were assigned to take care of the Tabernacle of Moses. In other words, it did not just fly up on its own. People assembled it and people attended to and maintained it. The Isaiah passage we have already discussed became alive in my mind at that same moment. *Yes, Lord! You do give and have given glory to our house!* I thought. *But I see how Your continued tabernacling among us is conditioned upon steadfast and prayerful worship maintaining the "tent."* I saw more clearly the priestly ministry of sustaining that dwelling as a responsibility fully incumbent upon *us*.

God has promised that His covering will be on every house where His people dwell and that the glory will be a protection for them. He has given every home the option of receiving and living in this benediction. But I was being reminded that it is not automatic. Spiritual covering must be maintained, and we who know Jesus Christ are the assigned priests of our homes, whose prayer-filled maintenance is essential to *sustain* the tabernacle of that home. If there is no one in a home who knows the Lord, of course, that mantle of protection does not exist. But if that covering is there by reason of the faith of even one person, *it needs to be maintained*.

I knew these things in theory before this. But that morning the Lord prodded my attention, helping me focus on a neglected area and recognize what action I needed to take.

First, I prayed.

I began to bring before God's throne each of those areas of concern I saw as essential for the moment. What I had sensed under the tent were all those many friends and situations under the aegis of Anna's and my leadership, vulnerable to the elements of hell's fury if left uncovered by prayer. Everybody has such responsibilities. They are the people, places and things that depend on your caring and sustaining a basic mantle or "tabernacle covering" of loving over their lives and concerns. It may involve family, business or circumstances, but if you and I do not attend to our tabernacle, those things become exposed.

As I reviewed these matters of spiritual responsibility and duty before God in prayer, I moved toward a second action. In contrast to the spiritual issue of prayer, this action was a very physical one. Though it may seem peculiar to some, I felt it was something I was to do.

I have always been struck by the way C. S. Lewis ends his small book *The Great Divorce*. He describes his imagined vision of a scene depicting life as it is lived by each of us—seeing us as choice-driven pieces on a chessboard. Each human being in Lewis' vision is a small figurine like a chess piece, and towering above each piece is the real person—the spiritual entity who determines his or her own destiny. His point involves three things: (1) the proximity between the physical and the spiritual realms of our beings (they are not separate but integrated); (2) the enormity of the spirit compared to the body (it is not a phantom, but the "real" me—larger and more permanent); and (3) the issues our spirits decide (which are more than temporal, but are eternal in consequence). That picture of man as a spiritually decisive entity, painted so graphically in Lewis' words, was set profoundly in my mind, and became an integral part of the picture now rising in my own vision.

I stood with my feet on the living room floor, there in our home. But in my vision I saw myself much taller than our house. (Let me hasten to say that I viewed this as entirely imaginary, as Lewis' words were; I am not suggesting some transcendental experience.)

This height enabled me to encompass my dwelling within the embrace of my own reach. This was significant since I also saw myself equipped with a giant sledgehammer, and my house as a tent—with ropes loose, snapping in the breeze, the roof about to blow off. The "giant" size allowed me a circumference of reach and a leverage of action that was now to be applied. And it was there, as I bent forward in prayer beside the couch, that I went through motions of literally and physically (1) reaching; (2) refastening; and (3) pounding.

I *reached* for the ropes—identifying each one as an area of neglect that needed to be tied down in prayer and recommitment to covering.

I *refastened* each rope—praying in the power of the Holy Spirit for people, places and things I knew I was accountable to care for in prayer.

And I *pounded* with the hammer. I lifted the huge, invisible sledgehammer, and like a nineteenth-century layer of railroad ties, I drove the stakes more tightly into place at the corners of our property.

In the scene I was envisioning, it seemed as though I had been given the skill of a *ranchero* who could lasso at will whatever he wished. In acting out literally what the Lord was showing me, I hurled that rope toward the corner stake and it would catch the stake and whip around it. Then it was as though the hand of God reached down and tied the knot, and I could see each rope pulled firmly to tighten up the tabernacle.

With that accomplished, I now knew that one more thing remained to be done: The tabernacle needed to be filled with praise. I remembered seeing an enormous air tent some years before, the kind that had no poles, but was supported only by the presence of the air pumped into it. While it was not the same kind of tent as the one I was staking, I realized that the "breath of praise" was the key to keeping the tabernacle "full"—the key to a glory covering being reinstated and secured so that the strong winds of adversity could not dominate my house.

As I began to praise in quiet melody that morning, I knew He was raising up the fallen tabernacle. In the weeks that followed, practical points of recovery began to be made manifest:

- Nagging illnesses that seemed to hang on to family members disappeared.
- The general "unrest" that threatened to stampede us simply evaporated.
- Anna and I renewed our relaxed times of fireside conversation together.
- Things at the office settled into a more normal flow: We were not less busy, but we didn't feel swamped!

In other words, it seemed that as soon as the stakes of the tabernacle were pounded into place, the wind-snapped ropes fastened with prayer and the tent filled with praise, the other "pounding" stopped. There is a wearing, unending beating that comes when somebody's tabernacle ropes are loose and snapping. It is as though the frayed ends of those tent lines are loose wires in our nervous system, or whip cords flaying our souls. But once they are captured, tied and pounded into place through prayer and praise-filled response, the peace of God's presence will be restored.

Someone may ask if I believe the physical action accompanying the spiritual act of prayer was necessary or important.

I do not know if I can dictate to anyone else that such a response to God's dealings is necessary, but for me I know it was, and that it was important. It was necessary for me because I felt a clear prompting to "live out" the clear discovery I had made. And it was important because it was a reaffirmation of my conviction that the invisible and visible realms are not as separated as we tend to think. Just as surely as we link the invisible and visible in the act of water baptism when we put our faith in Jesus Christ, so I believe God would always have us remember that the spiritual and natural dimensions of our lives are completely integrated—like it or not. My action with the hammer and my reaching for the snapping ropes forged a connection in my spirit and my mind that became and continues to be unforgettable.

So if you choose not to take such physical action, I would not think you less spiritual than I, just as I do not consider myself less rational for having done so. I never believe that God's words to me must become binding on anyone else. For unless people feel a harmony of heart and a witness through the Word, they certainly need not do anything because I have suggested it. A word of God to my heart does not authorize me to manipulate anyone else, and I reject "prophets" who employ apparent or proposed supernatural insights to manipulate people.

This occasion of the tent and other episodes I have related are not offered to impress anyone, but (1) to describe how I was made sensitive to God's Spirit concerning matters of personal need; and (2) to encourage you to allow Him to speak to and shape *you*.

We all encounter "strong winds."

We all desire "glory" on our house.

We all want to expel the "leprous" from our dwellings.

We all want to keep in alignment with God's throne.

To realize the fulfillment of those desires and goals in our ongoing experience, we need to listen to God.

Listening to God

When I say "God speaks," I am making a specific statement predicated upon certain scriptural truths.

First, God speaks to everyone. Yes, He does—to every human being. He does it by means of both general and specific revelation. For example:

- The starry *heavens* bear testimony to His eternal power and Godhead.[4] Creation itself testifies to its Creator, which is the reason an internalized awe and "sense of God" moves us when we gaze at the night sky, ponder the relentless tides of the sea or look into a baby's eyes.

- Our *conscience* is an inner voice of God.[5] This secret point of inescapable awareness and accountability is present in one way or another with virtually every person. Conscience may be smothered and silenced—even seared or burned over. But it cannot be escaped.

- God speaks in the *Bible,* the written Word of God.[6] Here is the source of His clear and analyzable revelation, where propositional truth is synthesized and practical understanding made fully and accessibly available.

- God has spoken in His only begotten Son, *Jesus* of Nazareth. The character, actions, miracles, teaching, life and death of Jesus are all expressions of God's living Word. He has spoken in Christ—and continues to speak through the testimony of Jesus, which you and I bear to others.

- God speaks to people in the *church assembly,* as the Holy Spirit prompts someone with a word from the Lord.[7] Such subjective words must always remain in alignment with established principles of His timeless Word. The Spirit of prophecy speaks not by adding anything to the Scriptures, but by making the eternal Word of the Scriptures practical, powerful and alive to us at given points of needed understanding.

- He also speaks by the example of godly *relatives* whose

influence marks so many, through their character and by prayer.[8]

By all these means, then, no human being is exempt from experiencing direct messages from almighty God, to whom we will all have to give account. So I am not hesitant to say, "God spoke to me." Since He has communicated so fully and freely with us *prior* to our new birth, it should not be surprising to find that He *continues* to do so in even more personal ways once we become His children.

And yet when I say that the Lord has spoken to me, I mean something even more specific than general revelations or private inner impressions. I reserve these words intentionally for the rare, special occasions when, in my spirit, I have had the Lord speak directly to me. I do not mean, "I felt impressed," or, "I sensed somehow." Instead, I mean that at a given moment, almost always when I have least expected it, the Lord spoke *words* to me. Those words have been so distinct that I feel virtually able to say, "And I quote." Had anyone else been present, I doubt that they would have heard an audible sound, for such words—however specifically spoken—are still heard internally, in our "spiritual ears," so to speak. Nevertheless, we may say, "I heard the Lord speak."

I believe it is important to learn to hear and respond to such dealings of the Holy Spirit. This is precisely the meaning of the promise reaffirmed the day the Church was born:

> "And it shall come to pass in the last days, says God, that I will pour out of My Spirit on all flesh; your sons and your daughters shall prophesy, your young men shall see visions, your old men shall dream

dreams. And on My menservants and on My maid-
servants I will pour out My Spirit in those days; and
they shall prophesy."   "Acts 2:17–18

"To prophesy" includes *hearing clearly* from God,
aligning clearly with God, *understanding* God *clearly* and
acting or speaking clearly according to God's Word. In
other words, the Lord has revealed His desire that all His
sons and daughters—all who are faithful servants, committed to living according to His Word, His will and in
the power of His Spirit—should have both the internal
direction of His Spirit as well as the external guidance of
His Word, the Bible. But always remember, the latter—
the Holy Scriptures, His eternal Word—is final. Every
word of the Holy Spirit's prompting must be measured,
controlled and consistent with the conclusive authority of
the Word.

I hasten to add that I do not believe that God's word to
anyone elevates him or her above others. I also want to
say that, while God's direct involvement in our lives is
exciting and fulfilling, there must be a stronger foundation for us than that. Some people try to build their lives
on an exciting word that God spoke. But I recommend
that the one point to build on solidly is the word of Scripture and the truth of the Lord Jesus Christ found therein.
God wants to commune and communicate with all who
will seek Him in pure worship and holiness of heart (John
4:24; Jeremiah 29:11–13). He wants to lead us all, to
direct and bless us, to show us the way we are to go. If we
respond to the truth of the eternal Word, the Bible, any
present word or work of the Holy Spirit He wishes to
accomplish will best be actuated in us and advanced
through us.

To do this, God does not need to address us verbally each day, but there will be pivotal times in our lives when He will do exactly that. This is not the sole privilege of a select few, but neither is it a random action on God's part. He seeks those who seek Him, and He speaks when He has something distinct to say pertaining to that person's life and circumstance, just as He did to me that morning when we dealt with the spiritual covering of my home.

As it pertains to our homes, many of us are slow to respond, brushing aside that "still, small voice" that is ever ready to speak to us and meet us at any point of vulnerability and need. But the Lord calls us to be ever vigilant in regard to our homes. We face a relentless enemy. That is the reason the Bible shows us, and the reason why I urge you (and testify that I do), to keep open in prayer to the Holy Spirit's promptings.

A Case of Applied "Hearing"

In November 1987, our oldest daughter was preparing for bed one evening. Because Scott was out of town, Becki was going through the nighttime ritual of locking up the house and turning lights out herself. As she was double-checking on their children, looking in on the two boys, everything seemed fine.

Last of all, she went to check on their three-year-old daughter, Lindsey. After tucking the covers up around the sleeping child's chin, she turned to leave the room. As she did, macabre words came to Becki's ears: *Lindsey is going to die.* Not knowing what else to do, she turned back, laid her hands on Lindsey and prayed, "Lord, I don't know if You are giving us some warning about the safety of our daughter, or if the devil is trying to bring fear into our home. But I ask You now to protect Lindsey from anything or from any way Satan would seek to harm her—in her body or soul or spirit. In Jesus' name, Amen."

Having done that, Becki turned to leave the room. But again she was stopped with the words *Lindsey is going to die.* So once more she turned back to pray over the little girl. This happened two more times, and each time Becki returned to her knees to extend prayer over Lindsey. Finally, feeling released in her spirit, Becki went to bed, feeling so at peace about the situation that she forgot it completely and did not even remember to mention it to Scott upon his return home.

About the same time, though I was unaware of Becki's experience, I received a telephone call from our friend Stormie. (She and her husband, Michael, are one of our "elder couples.") I knew that Stormie prayed for our family every day and she told me now that each time she had prayed for us during the preceding week she had begun to weep uncontrollably.

Not knowing what was behind this and not sensing clearly in her spirit how she should pray, she said she began to ask the Lord to give her understanding. She relayed how the Spirit of the Lord had spoken these words to her: *Satan is trying to pierce Pastor Jack's heart.* She said she had pressed further in prayer, asking the Lord, "Does that mean he's going to have a heart attack? How should I pray?" The Lord responded, *Satan is going to try to pierce Pastor Jack's heart through one of the grandchildren.*

As she related this to me over the telephone, I could feel her deep concern. Knowing that she and Michael are sound believers and not given to superficiality or whimsy, I took her very seriously.

It's time for a family meeting, I thought.

Later that day Anna and I called all of our children. We scheduled a time to meet together and it was there that I related the incident to them. Our purpose was to gird up together as a family, especially to secure a prayer cover over all of the grandchildren over the next several weeks.

As we were all meeting together, Becki remembered what had happened in Lindsey's bedroom those few days before. She shared that with us and, although as a family we began to pray for all of the grandchildren, we felt that the Holy Spirit was focusing our prayer cover over Lindsey in a particular way.

This occurred in November, and with the Christmas season approaching, I decided I needed to clean out our garage. Several weeks had passed since our family meeting and prayer together and, though we were still praying, the tenseness of the warning did not seem as prominent.

I had come across a number of things in my garage clean-out that I thought our kids could use. So one afternoon I called them all, asking if they would like to stop by and select those items they would find useful. I was just finishing up the job when Scott and Becki, along with their three kids, stopped by. Scott helped me as I finished the sweeping, while Becki and Anna visited in the house. We thought the kids were inside watching TV, but somehow Lindsey had drifted back outside and was busy checking out whatever three-year-olds check out in backyards.

Because our hefty two-and-a-half-car-wide garage door

had a broken spring, I had propped it open with a pole. But now, having finished the broom work, I gave one last, quick glance around to make sure that everyone was out of the way before I dropped and closed the door. Just as it began to fall, from out of nowhere walked Lindsey, and that mammoth reinforced door began arcing directly toward that little tyke's head.

It is absolutely miraculous that I caught it!

I stopped the falling door, pushed the prop back in place and swept Lindsey up into my arms, trembling with shock, my eyes filling with tears. And in one revealing instant I knew what had happened. I turned to a shaken Scott with my eyes brimming and said, "That was it! That was what the Lord was warning us about!"

Believe me—we had a praise session!

Each one of us recognized that God had used Holy Spirit-prompted warnings to prepare us through vigilant prayer. Such warnings tend to frighten some people, but God's workings are not something to be feared. Contrary to some human responses, warnings are not "bad omens." Neither are such warnings to be seen as God's way of letting us know in advance of "something evil He has predestined." The Father does not predestine evil things toward us, but His Spirit does warn us of calculated attacks by the enemy. In this instance, I have no question whatever: God's grace and wisdom prompted a response that preserved the life of our granddaughter.

Praying for an Outpouring

But we are not just called to pray against the strong winds of curse that our enemy would design; we are also privileged to pray for the powerful winds of blessing that God wants to send like breezes of joy upon us.

It was early in the morning when I awakened. This was no "prompting"—just the peculiarities of sleep patterns being interrupted by jet lag.

I was in Manila, having come to the Philippine Islands to speak to a gathering of more than three thousand pastors from dozens of denominations. Even though my body was in the Far East, it insisted it was still time-tuned to the U.S. West Coast. Because my roommate was still asleep, I chose not to get up even though I was wide awake. So to avoid disturbing him, I remained lying there in the room's inky darkness and quietly began my morning prayer time. I intended to begin as I usually do: first praying for Anna and the children, and then moving on with prayer for our congregation as well as other matters occupying my heart and mind.

I had hardly begun to pray for our family, however, when as clearly as I have ever heard the voice of the Lord, He spoke to me saying: *Pray for an outpouring of the Holy Spirit upon your children and your grandchildren.*

As clear as the statement was and as strongly as it was engraved immediately in my heart, I was not impressed with any sense of urgency—only with a sense of special responsibility. This was not a directive received by reason of crisis, for I knew of and sensed nothing on the order of the desperate. While such a call could signal an emergency—our being in regular touch with all our kids—I knew this was not addressing an immediate difficulty. So I simply began to pray as the Lord had directed me, mentioning each of our children and grandchildren by name—all sixteen. There are our four, born into our home, and their spouses. But at that time there were also eight more—grandchildren spanning in age from one to nine years old. So I named each one of the sixteen children in direct blood relationship—praying for God to pour His Spirit upon each one of them. I asked that this working of God's Spirit be:

1. according to the capacity of each one to receive at this time, and

2. continuously in the years to come, as God's purpose unfolds in each life.

I continued this for the next several days. As I did, I began to realize that the directive given to me had more far-reaching ramifications. I sensed that God was calling me to begin praying for an outpouring of the Spirit on other sons and daughters, those who had been born into ministry through the life of our congregation. Not only are there well over a hundred couples who have been sent into ministry from The Church On The Way, but there are many others who have chosen to relate themselves to the life of our congregation—looking to us for supporting prayer.

Now, the ramifications of that word were continuing to grow, and with it an ever-broadening sense of mission to *act* and also *declare*. I felt deeply that I was not only to *pray* for the children—infants, toddlers, preschoolers, grade-schoolers and teenagers—but also to call those to whom I minister to do the same. I knew I was to call our people to pray for God's Spirit to be poured upon a rising generation: from their direct blood relatives to anyone they knew. It was becoming very clear: We were first to answer the Lord's call to accept our place as *recipients* of the blessing of the Holy Spirit's fullness, then to answer the Lord's call to our place as *participants* in the ministry of prayer, laying claim to God's blessing on every child we knew.

The personal implications of such praying were obvious:

- I must be committed to a Spirit-filled life, as one who is seeking God for such in others' experiences.[9]

- Such "outpouring" is God-intended today. There is nothing sectarian or sensational in the quest—it is biblical.[10]

- The purpose of the outpouring is to prepare a generation not only for daily living but for service to Christ as well.[11]

- The urgency of the summons invites insight into the reason for this prayer now—that the spirit of the last days will not be resisted successfully without the Spirit of the early days filling us to overflowing![12]

And that is why I conclude the personal section of this book with this story.

We are in desperate and ferocious times.

This is not a matter of pessimism or prophetic excitability. The raw reality of the days in which we live is pointing to a showdown between two spirits, two streams, two forceful winds.

First, the Holy Spirit of the living God is engaging all God's people with a renewing, reviving call to open to the glory of His grace in Holy Spirit fullness. The objective of this experience is not to introduce us to a glib, giddy kind of "charismania," but to equip, prepare and fortify us against the spirits of darkness, deception and destruction.

Such Spirit–filled saints are intended to be the Salt and Light Company of the end times, "doing business" until Jesus Christ returns.

> "So he called ten of his servants, delivered to them ten minas, and said to them, 'Do business till I come.' "[13]

Second, there are two streams traveling in diametrically opposed directions. There is the River of Life flowing from God into the inner man of those who believe in Christ,[14] and then overflowing through and beyond each of us to water a thirsty world. This river is refreshing for us, while it is also hastening the harvest of the last ingathering. But near at hand there is also the corrupted stream of the mindset and muddied morals of this present age. It sweeps multitudes away to confusion and eternal loss. But if those of us in the first stream keep our lives centered in this pure flow of God, a holy dynamic will be generated as the holy power of God's Spirit flows naturally from us. It will attract those sickened by the sour swill of the fouled stream from which they seek rescue, a stream that has sucked them dry while pretending to satisfy.

And finally there are two winds.

The Bible reports the Church's birth in Acts 2, and especially memorable is the mighty manifestation of the "rushing wind"—a symbolic evidence of the irresistible power of the Holy Spirit when He is welcomed into the hearts of earnest believers. In stark contrast to this holy wind, the book of Job describes an evil wind—a tornado-like burst that the observers attributed to God. But the context does not say that. The revelation of the Word clearly ascribes this to Satan's hateful assault on Job's family (Job 1:18–19). The story is more than a report of Job's trial: It is a picture of the heinous nature of the adversary we oppose and his style of seeking the destruction of God's purpose in His servants.

And it is as one of His servants that I write to you.

The purpose of describing the promise available to us all in God's promised glory, and His desire to visit that glory on your house, is that you and I may meet the forces converging upon us in these momentous times with the full adequacy of God's sufficiency.

The tabernacle is falling, the Spirit summoned. And I rose to confront hostile winds that would devastate, diminish and destroy.

Pray for an outpouring, He directed. So I sought Him with the awareness that these are days in which only the Holy-Spirit-filled shall be prepared to resist the hellish forces being arrayed.

Beyond the conflict, there is a fundamental beauty in it all.

God has never had a people who were at the mercy of circumstances. His wisdom always anticipates hell's worst and provides for heaven's best. So it is with high confidence that we may look to Him, notwithstanding the bleakness of the present scene surrounding us.

His blessings upon *you,* dear friend!

Walk in the fullness of His resources. And like Israel's people awaiting their day of deliverance in Egypt long ago, when the darkness could be felt and they "had light in their dwellings," the climate of the times will make no difference.[15]

We are the redeemed. Our future is kept in the hand of

Him who is our present and ultimate Deliverer. And regardless of the present darkness, He has bequeathed to us a living promise.

We can have glory on our houses!

Now and forever.

Notes

[1] Amos 9:11.
[2] Numbers 10.
[3] Isaiah 54:1–3.
[4] Psalm 19; Romans 1:20.
[5] Romans 2:14–15.
[6] Romans 10:17.
[7] 1 Kings 19:12–13; 1 Corinthians 14:1–5.
[8] 2 Timothy 1:5.
[9] Ephesians 5:17–19.
[10] Acts 2:38–39.
[11] Acts 1:5–8.
[12] 2 Timothy 3:1–9, 14–17.
[13] Luke 19:13.
[14] John 7:37–39.
[15] Exodus 10:23.

Part II

Glory in His Church

8

A Vision for "People" Ministry

It was Wednesday evening, the eighth of March—twenty years ago. It is hard to believe two decades have passed!

Exactly two dozen people were in the room—six of them family members—and the group seemed even smaller sitting in a church sanctuary with a seating capacity of more than two hundred! Nevertheless, an air of excitement was present because loving people were present, and they were people who loved the Lord, too.

The roots of any renewal in the Church always begin with people—people who will answer God's calling. And that is why Anna and I were sitting in the second row with our three older children (ages eight to twelve) nestled beside us; she was holding our eleven-month-old baby girl in her arms. We were there because we felt God wanted us to be.

Dr. N. M. Van Cleave, supervisor of the Foursquare Churches in the Southern California area, was there to introduce us officially as the new pastors of the Van Nuys congregation. It was a sort of homecoming for him and his wife, since they had pastored this church over three decades before during the more fruitful years of the congregation's life. Mrs. Van Cleave had already presented us privately to some of the dear elderly people who had gathered to greet us, for she knew most of them well from earlier years.

For only sixteen members to show up at a meeting like this might sound disappointing, but they were thrilled that "almost everyone" was present. In fact, only eighteen members remained in the tiny congregation at this time, but what they lacked in number and youthfulness they made up for in warmth and experience.

When I was introduced, I stood before them informally rather than walking to the pulpit. I smiled and said, "If no one minds, I would prefer to stand here for what I'm going to say."

No one did mind, of course, nor do I suppose that anyone really understood my point in placing myself there at the time, but I had a reason for positioning myself below the elevated platform that night we were introduced. I was determined that for however long I would serve these people, I would function from a new level of understanding about pastoral service; and my station at their level was a kind of announcement, no matter what kind or how high a platform the future might require.

None of us had the remotest dream of what began with my few remarks that evening. I had consented to come here on a temporary assignment, feeling led by God to accept Dr. Van Cleave's invitation to assist this declining church. It was a "help-out-on-weekends-and-midweek-services" proposition, and the challenge it offered seemed exciting, but I did not expect that we would be there for more than a year or so. By then my position at the college would be fulfilled, and Anna and I expected that we would be offered a sizable pastorate involving great opportunities. Our sense of mission here was simply to serve in the interim way we were requested to fill. And although I did not know it then, in the months to come God would shake me to the roots of my being. I would begin learning church life in dimensions inconceivable to me that evening.

Still, I did have a sense of Christ's desire to renew His Church around the world; and however short my term of probable involvement here, I wanted to test those possibilities that the Word of God held forth.

So I asked that handful of dear saints to read with me a passage from the New Testament:

> Not that we are sufficient of ourselves to think of anything as being from ourselves, but our sufficiency is from God, who also made us sufficient as ministers of the new covenant, not of the letter but of the Spirit; for the letter kills, but the Spirit gives life.
>
> 2 Corinthians 3:5–6

That evening's gathering was intended merely as a brief time for the new pastor to be introduced and to respond before we all retired to the basement fellowship hall for refreshments and personal greetings. But I felt I had to make two things clear from the beginning. Thus, my opening remarks as pastor of the First Foursquare Church of Van Nuys, California, occupied only the next few minutes.

"I have read this passage," I said, "because it sets forth a principle that I would like to govern our thoughts and our life together for however long the Lord Jesus wills Anna and me to be your pastors."

I proceeded to explain the context of the passage, and drew my group of listeners toward an observation that I myself had not understood until only a few months before. I had not seen how this text focuses on the ministry of every Christian. I remarked how every believer in Jesus Christ is promised a basic sufficiency for being and becoming everything Jesus wants him or her to be. And I added that He wants to enable us to be an expression of His life wherever we find ourselves.

No one seemed particularly impressed that night, nor did I expect them to be. The rich reality and realizable practicality of my words were not apparent at the moment. The proposition that "all of us are in this together" and that "I will be depending on you" tended to sound like diplomatic, proper remarks appropriate for any leader about to take office.

But that was not my motive.

"I see us as becoming a truly ministry-minded church," I explained. "The Lord Jesus Christ is our center. The Word of God is our base. The Holy Spirit, enabling us to extend the servant life of Jesus outward—that's our objective. And, praise God, this text assures us that He will make us sufficient to be and to become able ministers of this kind of New Testament life!"

I added, "This will not be a pastor-centered ministry but a people-centered ministry—all of us serving in Jesus' name." Nobody shouted, seemed surprised or flinched. I thought I understood what I was saying, though I doubted that they were getting it. Actually, we were all in for one holy surprise ahead. That would be years in coming, however, and this was only Day One.

A bit of background may be useful to give perspective on what followed then and what follows here.

When we first accepted this pastorate, I was serving as dean of students and member of the faculty at LIFE Bible College in Los Angeles. I was asked to take that position following five years as National Youth Director for the Foursquare denomination.

LIFE was Anna's and my alma mater. After graduation, we had begun our pastoring duties by planting a church in Indiana—and this time of ministry also included significant involvement in the regional Foursquare youth program.

The years between Indiana and this evening had been filled with responsibilities, studies and travels—experiences that helped equip us for what was about to happen. Through pastoral and faculty involvement, we had cultivated a grasp of the Word of God, accompanied by a strong background in Bible teaching and preaching experience. Besides this, our travels within our own denomination, as well as among many other groups, had given us a deep appreciation for the different streams of fellowship within the Church at large.

Furthermore, we had encountered the fact that by this time, two streams of the Holy Spirit's enterprise in the Church around the world were converging rapidly: the classical Pentecostal stream and the spiritual flow beginning to be called the charismatic renewal.

Anna and I both had been influenced by the Foursquare denomination, one of the older and more steadfast expressions of the Pentecostal revival circling the earth in the early 1900s. Anna was born in North Platte, Nebraska, and from infancy had been involved in that community's Foursquare church. My own denominational background was more varied, however, quilted with various patches added every time our family moved during my childhood and adolescence.

My parents' spiritual birth occurred when I was only a year old. Jack and Dolores Hayford had responded to the message "Whosoever Will, May Come," delivered by Pastor Watson R. Teaford at the Foursquare Church in Long Beach, California. A few weeks later, I was presented for infant dedication, according to the Scriptures, as my parents began to set their lives and home in biblical order.

In the coming years, I received my spiritual input and grew spiritually in various denominations, but it always occurred in a congregation where the Word of God was taught and where Jesus Christ was honored. My parents saw to that. I am indebted to God's providence for providing years of background in the Presbyterian Church, the Friends Church, the Methodist Church and the Christian and Missionary Alliance Church. Intertwined with these experiences were periods of attendance in a Foursquare church, when one was near. Through my exposure to historic Protestantism, contemporary evangelism and classic Pentecostalism, I gained respect for broad and blessed traditions across the face of North American Christianity.

With this combination of historic Protestant and Pentecostal church experience, we became attuned to the sound of new showers of blessing that the Holy Spirit rained upon God's people everywhere.

We understood the fear and resistance toward the charismatic renewal that many of our fellow Pentecostals shared with leaders in denominations that were even older. At times we had to admit that those fears were justified. Some charismatics exhibited a distressing spiritual gullibility and love for sensationalism. It was disturbing to see people falling prey to the same excesses and exaggerations that have betrayed the blessing of God upon earlier revival seasons in Church history.

But here we were now, at this new pastoral charge, and we approached it as a challenging opportunity to walk with wisdom during a pivotal time in the life of the global Body of Christ.

From the beginning, on one hand, I sought carefully to avoid a "Pentecostalized" religious or denominationalistic prejudice. On the other hand, I sought to be wary of a reckless bent toward the anti-institutional or hyper-spiritualized habits developing in parts of the charismatic sector.

For our part, then and now, we prize proven values rooted in the practice of the historic Church, and we welcome the benefits of renewal that the Spirit breathes upon God's people tirelessly as they keep open to regular renewal. Given the perspective provided by our background, we stepped into this pastorate and hoped for God's gracious workings.

We sought a fresh walk in the Spirit, but we recognized how easy it is to mistake novelty for newness. We also saw how easily pride can prompt an arrogant, anti-traditional stance, leading to a tireless quest to be "different" for difference's sake. But we were equally sure that while newness is desirable, sometimes older methods are better, and we were committed to avoiding "man-pleasing," whether that man was a staid traditionalist or a rank newcomer to Spirit-filled living. We wanted to find Christ's mind for His Church, and to see the Holy Spirit work in our assembly according to the Father's Word, will and way.

The New Testament speaks both positively and negatively about tradition. A comparison of texts will show this.[1] One passage warns against traditions that transgress God's Word, while another urges, "Hold the traditions you have been taught."

We are persuaded that not all church traditions are invalid, and that church forms inherited from the past require cautious and prayerful consideration before we attempt change. We are bold enough to challenge history, but wise enough to abide by its lessons, remembering the philosophic maxim "Those who do not learn from history are destined to relive its errors." Still, whenever we discover places where human or church traditions choke simplicity, we examine those practices in the Word, with much prayer.

We have fumbled our way forward, yet hindsight confirms that as clumsy and unsensational as the slow way was, it established sturdy foundations for lasting ministry. Together it seems we have learned a thousand lessons: in heart renewal through humility and repentance; in disclosing ourselves through open confession; and in opening ourselves up to Holy Spirit-ignited discoveries through the Word of God. The unfolding of the future was a succession of discoveries of New Testament Church-life principles. But the first lessons had started a couple of years before.

The Priority in Ministry

We were here in the new pastorate with a sincere desire to equip believers to minister the life and love of Christ with grace and ability.

By pure scriptural assignment, church leaders are commissioned to serve this objective, and it is hard not to accept a hierarchical role as a spiritual "professional." People expect the priest or "the Reverend" to substitute for their own spirituality. So it is a reconditioning process to see what the Bible says about Jesus' instructions to His Church leaders. They are to train *every* believer to do the work of ministry and to upbuild the Church:

> And He Himself gave some to be apostles, some prophets, some evangelists, and some pastors and teachers, for the equipping of the saints for the work of ministry, for the edifying of the body of Christ.
> Ephesians 4:11–12

It took a long time to understand this concept! The cultural habits I mentioned above were true of me, too, and the Holy Spirit was remarkably patient in teaching me.

My reeducation began one day when one of the older students at the college came to see me. He was filled with excitement. As he spoke, I was puzzled as he expressed his eagerness to begin his public ministry. "I'm anxious to get at it, Jack; to be an instrument in developing the capacity of every member of the Body for ministry."

The words were coherent but they conflicted with my past experience of the pastor doing ministering, not the laymen. I sensed his enthusiasm, but listened rather unresponsively. I was bewildered, but the Holy Spirit told me that the young man had struck a vein of truth. Still, for the life of me, I could not absorb it.

As he left my office, I assured him of my encouragement as he moved toward graduation. Yet somehow, deep inside, I knew something had been related to me that transcended my spiritual grasp.

I left that encounter feeling as if a key to the Church's fulfilling its calling had been spoken by God to teach me—and through a student of mine at that! But I felt I had flunked the first lesson. Embarrassing.

In my capacity as professor of evangelism at the college, I was asked by our denomination's leadership a year later to represent them at a conference on evangelism held by another denomination. There this concept was presented again:

The ministry of the Church is to extend through every member of the Body, assisted and released by pastoral and other leadership.

The Holy Spirit was beginning to get through to me! I suddenly saw it! My job was to help God's people "find where they fit" in the functioning Body of Jesus—His Church here and now! But by what process? The unusual outline of the conference helped jar me to full attention.

The first speaker startled me with a new idea: *Evangelism begins with worship.* The second speaker said that by focusing on prioritized worship, the Church must become an integrated fellowship. Only then—and much to my amazement—the conference theme topic was broached: direct outreach and evangelism.

As I sat there, something was happening to me. It was all starting to fit together.

The "subjects," or the principal players, in ministry are the laity.

The "sequence" of the priority of ministry understanding is that *evangelism follows worship and fellowship.* Evangelism, I now was able to see, was intended to be not the result of slavish programs or stylish preaching. Rather, it was intended to be the natural byproduct of the life of Jesus Himself flowing from a healthy Body of believers nourished through worship and fellowship.

My spirit witnessed to the truth, but my mind recoiled in doubt. I looked around me for confirmation in the response of others there. But most pastors present apparently were not on the same wavelength. They were in the stage I had been in during that conversation in my office a year before: chained to traditional ideas about the pastor's role and the church's program of evangelism.

The idea that evangelism should be performed primarily by laymen and that the pathway to evangelism begins with the worship and fellowship of the Church had been well outside my range of acceptance—beyond imagination. No wonder that at that moment, it seemed beyond theirs, too.

Worship first? Mysticism!

The people as the ministers? Anarchy!

Were it not for the fact that at that particular time I was not pastoring a church, I am not sure I would have seen it, either. Even if I had, I might have dismissed the idea. It is unsettling!

Before this, I viewed worship more as a periodic activity than the key to the release of the Church's power. And as for the idea of ministry given to the laity—well, frankly, it is threatening to think that your field of expertise might actually be anyone's (everyone's?) domain. It seemed tantamount to saying that the way to build a house is to give the tools to kids in the neighborhood and turn them loose on a woodpile. But as I spent time studying the Word of God, the Holy Spirit helped me absorb these concepts and understand their possible application.

First, I saw that every member of the Body has the potential to be—and should be fed and led toward functioning as—a fully equipped agent of Jesus Christ. To be called "a minister" of Jesus' life is accepted more easily when people see it not as a noun but as a verb. To "minister" seems religious until the idea connects. Think of yourself as being equipped with knowledge of CPR and encountering a drowning. That is what it means to be ready to "minister." You are there with Jesus' life-breath when people who have "gone under" need help. I saw the goal of equipping the people as a reachable one, predicated upon two propositions:

1.   No one's ministry can mature unless it is taught, trained and served.

2.   Christ has given us apostles, prophets, evangelists and pastor-teachers to do that task.

The picture was clearing up. This was not a threat to pastoral leadership, but a demanding, self-giving assignment. A person's years of study at college and seminary would not be wasted because of an anti-clergy movement preempting the need for trained pastors or church leaders, supplanted by a magically enlightened laity. No, indeed. Instead, the leaders were the key to the laity's release in ministry—in fact, absolutely necessary to it. But each leader would have to make that commitment.

As I reflected on this, it came down to one question: Would I be willing to do my job—train the congregation for the work of the ministry—if it meant I might end up out of work? Perhaps they could sustain the ongoing ministry of the church without me. Was I ready for that?

It may sound strange or dumb, but I wondered about that issue. I decided on a "yes" answer, whatever the risk. I remember telling Anna, "Honey, if this 'equipping people to minister' thing really works, I could be selling shoes in a couple of years."

I meant it. But I intended to pursue the vision whatever it cost.

I was not prepared, however, for two things—two things that removed my availability to the shoe industry.

First, I was not prepared for the growth we enjoyed. I had thought that church growth came through programs, promotion, goal-setting and busy-work. One had to pray, preach and read the Bible, too, I felt. But the key was working at it—especially on programs and publicity.

Instead, I was beginning to witness another kind of growth. It was the growth of people gaining God's viewpoint on themselves, on His love for them and on His purpose for their lives. The Word of God and the love of God were growing big people, the kind of people who enlarge everything around them.

The church began to grow—not all at once, but it did grow. And I began to find that even though the maturing ones did not need me as much as they once had, a new crop of people was rising that *did* need me. They were the babes in Christ, the newcomers into the congregation, the adolescents turning the corner into college/career years and early adult maturity. All of them needed what I had to give.

The other thing I was not prepared for was how much the new "ministers"—the laity—came to love Anna and me. As they grew, some of the people no longer needed us, having come to a point of stability, maturity and beginning ministry themselves. Yet they loved us, and it was a new dimension of love unlike anything we had experienced. It was the gift of a deep, committed quality of grateful love from people who realized we had poured something of our lives into theirs, and who now loved us in return.

With years of this behind us now, incredibly, they still do not tire of us—and we all continue growing, "from glory to glory, even as by the Spirit of the Lord" (2 Corinthians 3:18, KJV).

The leadership of the Body does require trained people, of course. It is not a compromise to tradition or carnal habit for a congregation to have a salaried staff of formally trained people working full-time to assist the congregation in the will and way of God's Word and purpose. The union of the two was demonstrated beautifully on a sign I found beside a church office recently when Anna and I visited the Presbyterian church in Carmel, California. It read:

· Church Staff

The Ministers: *Every Member*
The Assistants: [the pastoral staff was listed here]

In that same spirit we had established as our chief objective the development of each person as a minister. Consequently, the question of how that was done became the most pressing item on our agenda.

I came to realize that worship was not only the essential priority; it was the fountainhead of *everything*—God's presence, His power, the guidance of the Word, the healing of souls, bodies and families, and the evangelism of the lost.

Notes

[1] Matthew 15:2–11, with 2 Thessalonians 2:15 and 3:6, and Galatians 1:14.

9

The *Chabod* of God

"Glory!"

It may be an exclamation, a visitation, an inspiration or an illumination. It is the theme of this book and the theme of a thousand more. But with all that may be said about it, the glory of God is transcendent—completely beyond conclusive description.

How shall we try?

It is a horrible analogy, but has anyone asked you to describe the taste of chocolate lately? My point is made. With God's glory, however, we are dealing not with a special taste in the world of our senses, but with the truth of the essence of the universe's Ultimate Personality—its Creator of all things.

When I began to believe that the essential approach to evangelism was an awakened spirit of worship in the life of a congregation, I did not fully understand why. First, of course, my convictions about the priority of worship were grounded in the Bible. Study had made that easier to accept: "If I pursue worship as the basic priority, I won't be less of a soulwinner." My background was ingrained with a raised-in-evangelicalism concern for "reaching the world for Christ," and I was still nervous at times about "worship" even as I was led to emphasize and pursue it. I had asked myself, "Am I drifting toward a dreamy vision of misty-eyed mysticism—worship for its own sake?" But as I continued looking into the early Church's life in the book of Acts, I not only found solid and persuasive answers, but I marveled at how obvious it was—and why I had not seen it before or been taught this perspective.

1.   When three thousand souls were saved at Pentecost, the day began with a prayer meeting and proceeded to a Holy Spirit-empowered worship service: They all spoke "the wonderful works of God" (Acts 2:11). The "tongues" languages weren't preaching; they were praising! And this supernaturally inspired worship drew the crowd and created the opportunity for the preaching of the Gospel (verses 1–11).

2.   After that day, the pattern was established: The people were daily at the Temple "praising God" (2:47). Within this environment, they gained such favor among all the people that souls were added to the Church every day by the working of the Lord Himself (verse 41).

3.   The miracle at the Beautiful Gate occurred as Peter and John were on their way to worship (Acts 3). The lame man's healing, Peter's sermon and the mighty ingathering of thousands of souls were byproducts of men en route to a prayer gathering. They had set out to worship God but "found" a miracle moment of power evangelism—more by a divinely appointed "accident" than through their own purposing.

But besides these three cases, there is no more profound example of worship as the key to the early Church's discovery of God's methods than the one occurring in Acts 13.

A Visit to Antioch

It was in Antioch, the first center of continued revival among Gentiles, that "as they ministered unto the Lord, and fasted," Church history came to a pivotal point.

"Ministering to the Lord" is the term for the priestly worship of God,[1] a task entrusted to us all because the New Testament makes all believers "priests to our God."[2] It is clear that the words *as they ministered to the Lord* are meant to teach us: The Holy Spirit summoned Barnabas and Saul (Paul) into missionary evangelism while they worshiped with the brethren!

It is even more impressive to see the results of that worship service. Not only did the Gospel break through to the Roman world, but what began that day in Antioch actually set the course for the whole westward flow of history. Think of it! The fact that western civilization courses are offered today in colleges and universities everywhere is the result of a worship service at Antioch-on-the-Orontes nearly two millennia ago.

All this helped me see why ministry to the Lord was first—at the top of the ministry list for the Church. To my mind, it had always more logically followed evangelism. After all, I reasoned, "We have to get people saved first. We cannot prioritize the humming of hymns while the world goes to hell!"

Gradually, however, I began to see that my whole experience in the milieu of evangelical Christianity had evolved into a philosophy that made evangelism something of a substitute deity. For every practical purpose, evangelism mandated that the worship of the Church be directed to it. I began to note how every component of true worship had been conscripted subtly and offered at the shrine of the Church's soul-saving enterprise.

All *sacrifice* was for "the evangelism of the world."

All *surrender* was our dedication to "seeking the salvation of souls."

All *devotion* was to "reach the lost."

All *ministry* was to "get people saved."

I may sound iconoclastic, but the fact is, the idol of evangelism has distracted many of us from the worship of the living God. It was hard for me to adjust to these priorities:

- Our first sacrifice ought to be the sacrifice of praise;

- Our first work ought to be the humbling of ourselves in His presence.

Since the Bible says that "no flesh should glory in His presence,"[3] we might reassess how often our self-generated zeal for evangelism, however well-intended, has made God Himself secondary in our pursuits. But His glory was coming back into focus for me.

Gaining a Grasp of Glory

Chabod.

It began to well up in my soul. *Chabod*—the Hebrew

word for "glory." I wanted to grasp this idea. (*Chabod* is pronounced kaw*bawd,* the *k* or *ch* sound preceded by a rough-breathing, guttural intonation.) *Chabod* occurs in some derivative form over 375 times in the Hebrew Bible, and scores of these relate directly to God. It is a heavy word in more ways than one, since the root idea inherent within *chabod* relates literally to weightiness. It is that which provides the foundational definition of the word.

> Over against the transience of human and earthly glory stands the unchanging beauty of the manifest God (Psalm 145:5). In this sense *chabod* takes on its most unusual and distinctive meaning. Its force is so compelling that it remolds the meaning of *doxa* (the Greek word for "glory") from an opinion of men in the Greek classics to something absolutely objective in the [Scriptures].[4]

This observation, pointing to the objective value of God's glory, emphasizes how its grandeur vastly exceeds the subjective value of which a human being is capable of estimating. Who can measure God? His glory is not a calculable quantity. But we can worship Him. And worship progresses when people are led to seek and come to know Him.

The weight, worth, value and splendor of God—that is, of His Person, nature and being—are of inestimable worth. It is in this regard that we speak of the incommunicable or absolute attributes of God. These refer to those qualities of His Person that have no comparison, and certainly no equal, in either our humanity or the creation around us. These characteristics are impossible to implant into the nature of His creatures.

1. *His transcendence:* "Behold, heaven and the heaven of heavens cannot contain You" (2 Chronicles 6:18). The God who made creation does more than fill it to the utmost corner of the universe. He exceeds it as surely as He preceded it and will remain when it has disappeared. Herbert Lockyer said, "His center is everywhere—His circumference nowhere. How the immensity of God baffles human imagination and explanation!"

2. *His eternal being:* "Now to the King eternal" . . . "from everlasting to everlasting, You are God" (1 Timothy 1:17; Psalm 90:2). God is not only endless, He is without beginning. This staggering idea boggles mere human minds. No matter how far our imagination pursues the thought of tracing time forward or backward, we must—by reason of our finiteness—conclude our comprehension of "eternity" at some point. But He never does. He never began. He will never end, either.

3. *His unchangingness:* "I am the Lord, I do not change" . . . "You (Lord) are the same" (Malachi 3:6; Hebrews 1:12). God's immutability describes both the fact that He has not changed as well as the fact that He will not change. I do not mean to attribute stagnancy to Him, as though His "unchanging" were the same as human boorishness or unimagination. Rather, it describes a constancy that is due not only to His absolute reliability, but to His total completeness. No change can be made because He is already complete. Entirely so.

4. *His self-sufficiency:* "If I were hungry, I would not tell you; for the world is Mine, and all its fullness" (Psalm 50:12). The completeness of His being ensures the absolute adequacy of His Person. God does not *need* anything. Whatever He asks of or calls forth from us is

only because He seeks to open something of His fullness of being to us and thereby release an abundance of His goodness in and over us. This incredible fact exists in His love: Even though He needs nothing, He still desires our fellowship.

5. *His omnipotence, omniscience and omnipresence:* "Great is our Lord, and mighty in *power;* His *understanding* is infinite.... Where can I go from Your Spirit? Or where can I flee from Your *presence?*" (Psalm 147:5; 139:7). These three attributes are the ones mentioned most frequently, those that conclude general listings of God's seven absolute attributes. These "omnis" mean He is *all*-powerful, *all*-knowing, and always—*everywhere*—present. This last trait, His omnipresence, differs from His transcendence. *Omnipresent* relates to God's presence within His own creation's boundaries, while His transcendence relates to His exceeding creation itself.

It is important to understand that God's presence within the realm of creation does not mean that He is within the created things themselves. That erroneous idea is called pantheism, which means that God is all things, rather than the Maker of all things. Other than the fact that He has chosen to place His own Spirit within His redeemed sons and daughters, God is not "in" created things. The notion that God may be worshiped in the trees, the seas and the loveliness of nature is pagan, for that worships the creation instead of the Creator Himself (Romans 1:18–25).

It is exhilarating to contemplate the splendor of God's nature—His personality.

Such an examination of the biblical revelation of God's Person and nature is important to our worship, especially today. In every era there have been diluted, popularized notions about God, but at few times in history has it been so widely supposed that humans are virtually "gods" themselves. This is the core doctrine of humanism: God is all and man is God. The supplanting of God's eternal glory and revealed truth with man's temporal being and finite opinions lies at the center of the present delusion causing the corrosion of culture. It also explains the arrival at *Empty* flashing on the soul's dashboard when we travel too far without God.

What Worship Brings

It is into this arena of humankind's emptiness and quest for meaning, direction and fulfillment that we have been sent by our Lord Jesus. It is not trite to say it again: Jesus Christ is the answer. But what can we do to cause blinded, empty souls to see and believe it? Their emotions are jaded. Their minds are blinded. Their spirits are dead. Their bodies are dying. Only an encounter with God's supernatural presence can address this dimension of need and impress the walking dead with resurrection life and power.

That is why worship must precede evangelism:

Worship is the *fountainhead* from which the redeemed drink to sustain the fullness qualifying them as visible witnesses to the reality of the living God. It prepares them to demonstrate Him through lives breathing of Him.

Worship is the *atmosphere* in which the unconverted, when welcomed, will "sense" the dimension of the greatness of the One whom they unwittingly seek. When the worshiping congregation is at its first task, worship, and doing it through the Holy Spirit's power, God's presence invading their midst will be convincing and compelling. The *chabod* of His presence draws the hungry soul to desire the true and living God.

Worship is the *testimony* that Jesus is alive, for as the living Church praises Him, the Holy Spirit's commitment to exalt Christ brings His presence with power. His working brings an intuitive awareness to those outside Christ that (a) Jesus Christ is truly real—alive; (b) He is God the Savior; and (c) only He can answer their need and bring forgiveness and life.

"I will glorify the house of My glory," the Lord promises, adding, "I will make the place of My feet glorious" (Isaiah 60:7, 13). Here God declares His readiness to pour the weight of His worth and working into the midst of the place we worship. As He does, people will be changed— impacted by the weight of God's *chabod* in that setting. Saints and sinners alike need it: The lightness, insufficiency, inadequacy, superficiality, emptiness and neediness in us all cries out for glory.

- The weight of God's glory is the only *worth* that can bring true self-worth.

- The weight of God's glory is the only *wealth* that can bring true abundance.

- The weight of God's glory is the only *force* that can tip the scales and turn the tide of human circumstance from emptiness to fulfillment.

The *chabod* of God is the ultimate reality. The only thing causing the slowness of human response is the residual human arrogance latent or active in us all. It is manifest in the mentality that somehow our visible realm is the "real" one, while the invisible realm is not quite as real—if it even exists. Even we believers reveal this propensity for confusion! How seldom it occurs to many that what is invisible to our gaze and intangible to our touch "just might be" a realm greater than ours.

Of course it is! Logic dictates it. The invisible realm is greater than the visible, by the simple fact that this transient visible realm came out of the invisible realm. The lesser follows the greater. And it is from that greater realm that the *chabod* of God—the weight of His glory—flows to ours. It flows readily and freely wherever worshiping souls learn that the fountain for their life, the wisdom for their minds and the strength for their souls come from God alone. As worship rises, His glory descends; the glory of His "ultimately real" world invades our so-called "real" world.

The "Weight" of Worship

During worship the Holy Spirit reveals Jesus, who is Himself the image of God's glory. With Him comes the full essence of His working that brings substance—weight—to our living. Through Him we learn to live in God's glory and begin to realize the practical benefits of the "weight of His glory."

- That "weight" will keep the soul from being blown away by the winds of adversity or error.

- That "weight" will anchor a marriage and keep it settled in love's commitment.

- That "weight" will flow into life's daily details and bring substance exceeding the frothiness of the present order.

- That "weight" will balance the accounts and neutralize the pain and pressure brought on by bitterness and temptation.

People who worship realize the "weight" of God's *chabod,* and become people whose lives and living define what holiness is about. Holy people are the result of God's transmitting His wholeness and completeness into their emptiness. Whatever their limitations due to sin or human weakness, they have come to their Creator for completeness and forgiveness through His holy Son. Into these, the weight of His glory brings substance to life, love to relationship, truth to all interaction and power-with-grace to all they touch.

God does not seek a holy band of worshipers in order to stage a parade of the religious. He wants a polluted, re-constituted, "now-we're-whole-again!" people through whom He can move to touch a pain-filled world. And this kind of people "happens" through their contact with Him.

"Enter into His presence with thanksgiving, and into His courts with praise!"

This breakthrough of praise into His presence not only evicts the enemy's badgering, but erects a dwelling place for God's presence to come to us in power. That is why He calls us to worship. He wants to meet with us and move among us; He wants to ignite the transformation of His people and initiate their interaction in His love. Worship in God's mind is intended for encounter and action. He wants us to know He is neither inaccessible nor impersonal. He is there—and He wants to be invited here to do something to us, in us and among us. His weight of glory does these things.

This idea was foreign to me.

Like some churchgoers who define worship as "proper," but whose expectations exist at less dynamic levels, the *chabod* of God for me involved something to affirm, not experience. For many of us, worship means meditation and contemplation, or culture, or education. Or perhaps an opportunity for personal inspiration and public affirmation—a restatement of one's faith. But however valid any of these thoughts on worship may be, or however worthy their net result, they do not accomplish the central revealed purpose of worship that God discloses in His Word.

God provides worship as the means by which a place is prepared for Him to meet and move among His people.

In both Old and New Testaments, God's revealed will in gathering His people is that we might experience His presence and power. This is not for spectacle or sensation, but for discovery and the realization of His will through encounter and impact. Such worship times will beget new capacities for effective living and a deeper confidence for practical and powerful spiritual service. The Father's desire when people worship Him was made clear when He directed Moses to build the Tabernacle. And from that time on, the Scriptures witness that the purpose is just the same.

- "Let them make Me a sanctuary, that I may dwell among them . . . and there I will meet with you, and I will speak with you . . ." (Exodus 25:8, 22).

- "Where two or three are gathered together in My name, I am there in the midst of them" (Matthew 18:20).

- "In [Christ] you also are being built together for a habitation of God in the Spirit" (Ephesians 2:22).

- "You also, as living stones, are being built up a spiritual house, a holy priesthood, to offer up spiritual sacrifices acceptable to God through Jesus Christ" (1 Peter 2:5).

In every age He has said, "I want to come in personal power and live where you are!"

These references apply to both believers' gatherings and more personal settings. But such words as *together* and *in the midst* seem most pointedly to include corporate gatherings—whether massive congregations or small home groups. As we come together, God says His express purpose is to make us a dwelling place—a place where the weighty *chabod* of God can come to abide.

The Way We Worship

Worship is for God. It is birthed by His gift of life to us and His great love for us. And worship is due Him and entirely for Him. Our passion in worship ought *never* to be tempered by a quest for the praise of men or gauged by our own personal preference.

How does He instruct us to worship Him?

His counsel in this regard under the Old Covenant was exact. Although those elaborate rituals are no longer required, they demonstrate that God makes the rules regarding proper worship. The demanding designs He draws are ones that call us back to childlikeness—to sing happily, to rejoice openly, to reach worshipfully, to cry humbly, to shout triumphantly, to praise unreservedly, to applaud appropriately—to come before His throne with a full sense of His worthiness and a judicious sense of our happy privilege to be invited.

Refusing the humility of a childlike approach before Him sacrifices the blessing of His fullest presence in power. We must realize this or else lose the blessing of His glory among us.

The New Testament reveals worship as more than a cerebral pursuit or a heightening of mystical consciousness. It is no more an intellectual exercise than it is an emotional binge. In God's order, worship brings man's total being aglow in the life that the Holy Spirit imparts, enabling him or her to offer spiritual sacrifices. Listen to the apostle Paul appealing for the complete human being to answer its summons to worship:

> I beseech you therefore, brethren, by the mercies of God, that you present your bodies [physical worship] a living sacrifice [emotional worship], holy, acceptable to God, which is your reasonable [intelligent[5]] service. And do not be conformed to this world [which devalues the worship of God], but be transformed by the renewing of your mind [thinking on God's terms, not your own], that you may prove [i.e., discover] what is the good and acceptable and perfect will of God.   Romans 12:1–2[6]

The Greek *proskuneo* (worship) means "to prostrate oneself before God," so humility is at the heart of true worship. This issue focuses not so much on physical prostration as it does on true prostrating of our pride before Him. Physical prostration during worship is certainly appropriate, but church architecture as well as social propriety make it impractical. And yet how changed we all might be this Sunday if our private devotions this week included prostration before God's throne!

Whatever the setting, we need to lay low our human wills before Him; to let childlike brokenness and obedience be demonstrated openly by our submission to His way in worship. Any human insistence on "my dignity" is unworthy. It is frothy stuff before the *chabod* of God! Fearful reserve in the name of my cultural taste must be challenged. May the Holy Spirit deliver us from such temptations to rationalized vanity, teaching us that

> *man's highest dignity is in the nobility of humbling himself in childlikeness before the King of the universe!*

Let us praise Him! Thank Him! Laud Him! Adore Him! And give Him place in our hearts and our churches for His glory to dwell in our midst.

An Addendum

The following categories and references serve as introductions only in this simple outline, but as we have led people in examining and exercising these and other significant biblical guidelines to worship, we experience the benefits of obedience. The issue is God's glory, and the outflow is His Kingdom, here and now!

Let us then worship[7] . . .

- With a Regenerated Spirit (Romans 1:9)

1.   Worshiping in the Spirit (John 4:23–24)

2.   Singing spiritual songs (Colossians 3:16; Ephesians 5:19)

3.   Giving thanks "well" by the Spirit (1 Corinthians 14:15–17)

• With a Renewed Mind (Philippians 2:3–5)

1.   Worshiping with obedient intelligence (Romans 12:1; 2 Corinthians 10:5)

2.   Praying with the understanding (1 Corinthians 14:15)

3.   Praising with the understanding (Psalm 47:6–7)

• With Revived Emotions (Colossians 3:23; Romans 12:11–15)

1.   Shouting and clapping hands unto the Lord (Psalm 47:1)

2.   Praising Him aloud with the congregation (Psalm 47:1)

3.   Rejoicing and expressing thanksgiving (Psalm 100:1, 4; Philippians 4:4)

4.   Being silent before the Lord (Psalm 46:10; Habakkuk 2:20)

• With a Rededicated Body (1 Corinthians 6:19–20)

1.   Kneeling in worship (Philippians 2:9–10)

2.   Bowing heads (Micah 6:6–8)

3.   Raising heads (Psalm 3:3–4; Hebrews 4:16)

4.   Lifting hands (Lamentations 3:40–41; Psalm 63:3–4)

5. Waving hands in praise (Leviticus 9:21)

6. Dancing with joy before the Lord (Psalm 30:11; 149:3; 150:4).

Notes

[1] Exodus 28:3–4, 41.

[2] 1 Peter 2:9; Revelation 1:6;5:10.

[3] 1 Corinthians 1:29.

[4] Harris, Archer and Waltke, *Theological Wordbook of the Old Testament* (Chicago: Moody Press, 1980), p. 427.

[5] The Greek *logiken latreian* includes both the enlightened reason and reborn spirit (*sic loyikos,* Arndt, Bauer, Gingrich, *Lexicon*).

[6] cf. Hebrews 13:15; 1 Peter 2:5; Psalm 51:17.

[7] From "The Way We Worship," a series of six messages brought to the congregation of the First Foursquare Church of Van Nuys, Cal., by Pastor Hayford. The tapes of those messages are available through SoundWord Tape Ministry, 14300 Sherman Way, Van Nuys, CA 91405. (Pastors and church musicians may write for information on tapes of leadership seminars on worship and for musical resources for teaching and leading worship.)

10

Breaking Out of Poverty

Poverty is more than not having *some*thing. It's a spirit that is always *fearful* of not having anything at all. The spirit of fear that affects the entire human race is so massive a force that even a person who has much still tends to think it will never be enough.

We are born crying, with arms outstretched and fingers clutching—grasping for something, even though we don't know what we want. Although mind and body develop, and tears and tantrums come under reasonable control, only a work of grace can remove our insatiable sense of needing to *get*, to *have* and to *keep* for ourselves.

I did not recognize how this mentality had characterized my own pastoral work and church leadership. Whatever I might have noticed, I probably never would have defined as fear, for the self-protectiveness begotten by the spirit of poverty is usually different from terror or panic, and the kind of selfish concern it produces is not greediness. But even though this unperceived reaction to the fear/poverty syndrome is not as hateful as stinginess, it still can bind us as badly. I was embarrassed to realize how much more motivated I was to get than to give, yet the trait had become well-masked in peculiar and seemingly spiritual ways.

In my first pastorate, for example, I did door-to-door work believing sincerely that I was pursuing a Christ-honoring search for the unchurched. God allowed us graciously to see a few souls brought to His Son through those efforts, but at this stage of self-perception, I was surprised by an honest self-assessment. I now realize that I was more concerned with my pastorate's growth than I was with the compassion Jesus showed:

> But when He saw the multitudes, He was moved
> with compassion for them, because they were weary
> and scattered, like sheep having no shepherd.
>
> Matthew 9:36

To what degree had love stirred my outreach? And to what degree was I moved by a fear of failure? The answers are not easy, and I do not intend for any of us to nitpick our motives until they bleed. But the point is made.

Another trait of this order of fear—the fear of "not having"—manifested itself when visitors came to visit our services. I was slow to see how easily I submitted to the temptation of catering to these guests at the expense of a genuine "pastoral concern." I rationalized my words and style as "being diplomatic," but I was concerned more with presenting "a pretty face" for our church, than with asking the Spirit how I could best serve the need of those with whom I spoke. I think that I was, in fact, more dishonest—motivated by the fear of not being able to "gain a crowd" unless I "charmed" people, rather than simply caring for them. My background and professional experience taught me how the casual modification of some remarks could provide a better image of the church—one that might persuade a visitor's continued attendance. But I found that while promotional banter, slick presentations and glad-handed superficiality might gain someone's membership, it will never cultivate people of strong character and true commitment. People won to a church by slick style tend to be slippery themselves. They will "slide" somewhere else when tough times come or when loyalty is tested. The evidence of such poverty-mindedness—the fear of not getting—exposed itself eventually in my thought patterns and terminology. The precipitation point for this self-discovery came one Sunday shortly after we came to Van Nuys.

A handsome family of five were visiting—Dad, Mom and three sharp kids. As a result of information I gained while conversing with them following the service, I remarked to Anna on the way home, "Wouldn't it be nice to get them into the church? We sure could use a family like that!"

Instantly, the Holy Spirit stung me—using my own words.

That episode marked the beginning of His helping me see by letting me hear myself.

Get.

Use.

Suddenly I was smitten with a shameful awareness. For the next several days I reflected on what I had said, grieved at what seemed like a dozen other behavioral patterns forged into my habit and fired by the spirit of poverty.

Poverty—the fear of not getting, of not having—had to go. Faulty material in the foundation of any life, once discovered, needs to be dredged out, removed at any cost. So I submitted to God's Holy Spirit. I realized that no true building of the Church of our Lord Jesus Christ is aided by scheming, marketing, promoting, public relational "slick" or by any concern preoccupied with getting. I learned that I cannot partner with Christ in His building of the Church if I have clutching hands.

And therein lay a further discovery. My faulty perception of church growth lay in my failure to see—or truly believe—that not only is Jesus the Church's Foundation, He is also her Architect and Builder. "I will build My Church," He announced on a mountainside in Galilee long ago. Now those words were engraved on my soul as the Spirit of God was pressing Jesus' personal pronoun into my awareness. It was, "*I* will build . . . I *will* build . . . I will *build!*" It was all His and of Him.

Things were changing. I experienced victory over the spirit of poverty, even though I did not know that was the culprit. These points of refined understanding helped me to see that fruit and fruitfulness were beyond my grasp anyway, so I could quit grasping. Desperation—however quietly controlled or carefully veiled—gave way to restful dependence on the Lord of the Church to grow her . . . and to grow me. It was nearly two months later that a barrage of basic principles about Jesus' ways with His Church and its leaders burst upon me. Included was a perspective on finances that launched an ongoing liberation process inside me and that soon came to rule the hearts of the leaders within our congregation.

A Late Night Encounter

It was now past one o'clock in the morning. As I sat in our living room rocking chair, I wrapped my bathrobe around myself against the late-night chill as I was waiting on the Lord in prayer. At one point, as I paused in my intercession, the Lord asked a question with crystal clarity. It seemed a strange one, peculiar to me.

You don't believe you're in My will, do you?

I could not have agreed less or been puzzled more. Why, I did believe I was in His will. Yet His question was suggesting—no, asserting—that I did not, not really. I kept my mouth shut and my mind open. He spoke again to my waiting heart.

Do you believe you are to be pastoring?

I nodded affirmatively, as though He were seated across from my chair.

Do you believe you are to pastor in Van Nuys?

Again I affirmed as much.

Do you believe you are to pastor the Van Nuys Foursquare Church?

Of course I did! What kind of quiz was this? God had suggested I did not believe I was in His will, yet everything He asked I was affirming.

And then came the punchline—a knockout blow leaving me flattened—in complete analytical disarray:

You believe that being in the Foursquare denomination is your own idea.

My mind reeled. A dozen streams of thought converged at once. For the next several moments I attempted to sort them out.

It was true, even though I had never perceived it in those terms. I *was* in the Foursquare denomination. I was not unhappy about it. And neither was I thinking of leaving for another group nor planning to take an independent posture.

But upon analysis, I realized I *did* believe "being Foursquare" was my own decision. I had come to a Foursquare Bible college for training years before, and the natural flow of events seemed to draw me into that fellowship.

Sure, I guess I did think it was a matter of natural choice. I mean, after all, isn't being in a particular denomination anyone's own decision? Surely God does not care which you choose. I mean, He is basically indifferent to the whole ecclesiastical hodgepodge, and cares only about people, not church groups, and. . . .

And now my thoughts were interrupted by a revelation from God's heart to mine. He showed me that I did not truly believe it was His will for me to be in the Foursquare Church. Suddenly I saw the picture. How dumb of me! How ludicrous to suppose that I could claim to be in God's will while pastoring the Van Nuys Foursquare Church if the "Foursquare" part was immaterial to Him! They were two parts of an inseparable proposition—the church, the denomination and God's will for me were one and the same. *Amazing,* I thought, *that this obvious fact has been wholly imperceptible to me until this moment.*

Further, the Holy Spirit flashed into my consciousness at that same instant that He was calling me to understand another fact. Since God placed me in the denomination, that made it a matter of obligation to Him, not man, that I participate in the policies of my denomination's ways of operation.

I am not saying that God said the Foursquare denomination is right in every policy or procedure. I am sure no group is, and while every church or group seeks to structure itself according to New Testament Church methods, we would be wise to admit there is no conclusive polity on ecclesiastical structures in the Scriptures. The focus is more on the character of leaders than on the construction of an organization. Debates on Congregational, Episcopal or Presbyterian forms of church government or questions concerning whether deacons, elders or trustees should lead the church, or whether a congregation should use literature from the presses of its denomination exclusively, or which parachurch organizations are justified and which are not—all such debate is so much rhetorical rummaging.

God could not care less about our self-justifying arguments. His question to me boils down to this: *Do you function in a spirit of submission and loving self-giving in the circle of fellowship where He has placed you?*

That night the issue was solved for me. He hit me between the eyes because I was *not* functioning in that way. I had not been making trouble, arguing or sowing discord among our denomination's brethren. My not-seen-till-now unwillingness to submit, however, showed up in a practical way. It was reflected in my partial participation in the financial program of the Foursquare Church. Let me explain.

Our denomination funds its offices, programs and church expansion by a monthly "extension tithe" from the member churches. This guideline calls for each participating church to send ten percent of its general tithes and offerings each month to the regional office of the denomination. (Missionary offerings and specially designated funds, such as building or developmental gifts, are exempt from the extension tithe.)

Although the corporate bylaws of the denomination show this tithe to be a required point of participation, local pastors over the years have varied widely in the degree of their participation. Thus, the extension tithe has become a voluntary matter (and no one was disciplined for not participating in the program, though many sent less than the full tithe expected). I was not alone in this limited pattern of cooperation: I had acquired it from the majority of pastors in our fellowship.

The bitter pill God was having me swallow was that, even though we sent a token tithe of $100 per month to our regional office, our church's monthly income (then about $2,500) warranted a lot more. This tokenism, while not uncommon at the time with other Foursquare congregations, caused me to rationalize this practice. But the rationale was gone: It was so stupid of me!

What a ridiculous term, *token tithe*. Imagine Abraham saying to Melchizedek, "You know, sir, the plunder from this victory is so great that it seems unreasonable to give you a full tenth. If you please, I think I'll simply give you this token, which I think you'll agree is quite sizable enough."

It is sadly laughable, for the Bible says that Abraham, in whose footsteps of faith the New Testament tells us all to walk,[1] "gave him a tithe of all."[2]

Not only was I corrected regarding my leadership, I saw that whatever "spirit" governs the leader will determine the mood of the whole congregation! First, the poverty spirit lured me to rationalize a withheld tithe, motivated by the fear "We won't have enough," and the loveless, vision-warping fruit of fear, " 'They' don't need that money anyway." My own submission to God was confronted and reinterpreted in a most brutal fashion. It involved more than my response to Him; my submission in His eyes involved my response to my circle of fellowship. And if my fear of "not enough money" and my fear of "not enough personal freedom" was not broken, the trickle-down effect of my disobedience would infect our congregation. They could be enlarged or hindered by my response.

Over years of ministry I noted a general principle. It does not explain all church problems, but I am convinced that many conflicts within congregations are but the sad projection of a pastor's own lack of submission to some aspect of God's will in his own life.

From the Top Down

Psalm 133 celebrates the blessedness of believing brothers and sisters dwelling in unity, declaring that unity is "like the precious oil upon the head, running down on the beard, the beard of Aaron, running down on the edge of his garments" (vv. 1–2). Before this encounter with the Lord I had not captured the obvious lesson:

Unity flows from the head!

I cannot expect any more unity, giving, love, submission, service—anything—in my congregation than I exhibit in the way I obey God myself. How I lead my household in love and peace will reveal itself in the church. My attitudes toward those whom God has placed over me in government, be it civil or ecclesiastical, will duplicate themselves in the way the people I lead generally respond to me. It is the inevitable law of sowing and reaping: You get what you plant!

As I have said before, I do not mean that God endorsed our denomination's financial plan as superior to any other group's. What He taught me, however, is that the imperfection in all human government can be compensated for only by His grace. That means that it is not my call to try to control a program I see as imperfect by trying to "save it" by my noncooperation. It is a "works" theology that tries to work righteousness where only grace in participation can accomplish the goal. When those within a given group submit graciously and lovingly to the methods of operation by which they are governed, it opens the door to the richest dimension of God's grace to flow. It would be wise for all church leaders to perceive this. God's government is "in spirit and truth." It is not perfected in the hands of legalists, but in the hearts of free and loving people.

As a result of this late-night encounter with the Lord, I asked the men of our church council to meet with me. I told the council how I now had come to believe that we should bring our church's tithe to headquarters to a consistent tenth. As I related God's dealing with me on this matter, I went on to explain how our denomination had taken the principle of the tithe from Numbers 18:26. Here the Lord told Moses to require the Levites to offer a tenth of the tithes they received to Him (see also Nehemiah 10:38). In other words, there was a biblical precedent for the concept of a "ministry tithing on its tithes" and ministering them at another level.

But there was a New Testament principle at stake also:

> Let every soul be subject to the governing authorities. For there is no authority except from God, and the authorities that exist are appointed by God. Therefore whoever resists the authority resists the ordinance of God.   Romans 13:1–2

When I expressed my deep feeling that God had summoned us to manifest our submission to those authorities placed over us in family association, the brothers con-

sented heartily. It was a joy to witness *their* submittedness, and the next day we paid our tithes—in full. We
went retroactively to the preceding month, and from that
day to this we have given it as a faithful minimum—an
amount I might add that under God's blessing now runs
presently to nearly a million dollars in tithe per year as
God has blessed our people abundantly.

With that decision, it seemed as though a lid came off.
An entirely new, freeing viewpoint captured my mind,
and the liberty it brought swelled within the hearts of
those in our congregation. While every congregation
must attend to its basic financial needs, we realized that
our largest responsibility was to be available prayerfully
and to give unselfishly. The giving was more than mon-
etary. It affected other attitudes of selfishness we had
failed to recognize.

Take the issue of those who wanted to leave our church
to join another. Instead of allowing a disapproving or
accusing mood that forced a secretive "side-door" exit, we
taught people to be unafraid about their decisions. Members of the congregation were free to express to the pastor
or elders their sense of God's direction if they felt drawn
to another assembly. "It's Jesus' Church," we taught
them, and encouraged them to obey if they felt led elsewhere. We began to take delight in sending people
forth—letting them go with our blessing. It allowed them
to depart with a positive sense of God's purpose and ministry rather than being saddled with guilt for leaving.
Our will to function in this openhanded spirit was no less
gracious when folks expressed their plans to attend a
congregation of another denomination.

And as we served and gave more and more, doors of

opportunity opened more and more, making room for God to show His hand of power and provision through us.

The giving and growth of the congregation increases continually without promotion or intense programming. I teach about two Sundays per year on giving, but otherwise little is said about the offering. Now the multimillion dollar budget we administrate annually allows us expanded means for evangelism, including a missions budget of over two-and-one-half million dollars per year. Hallelujah! The Lord never calls us to learn His ways without offering His life in return!

To all of His own who will commit to covenant with the Lord in their giving, He gives great promise. We have sought to walk a balanced line in teaching and living in this blessing of His promise—His promise not only of abundance, but of protection.

I had heard how Galatians 3:13–16 reveals that those who come into covenant with Jesus Christ are Abraham's seed by faith. As "Abraham's seed," we put our emphasis on obedience to God, not formulas for faith, and that means that what God promised to Abraham—the blessing of His grace and the blessing of His abundance—becomes ours by grace also as we, like Abraham, walk in the covenant that God makes with us.

At first, I resisted this teaching because I saw some who exaggerated its application. But I decided to teach the truth and then model its balance by our mood and manner in the life of the congregation. It worked, and we began to see growth in faith for giving, but still we avoided equating wealth with godliness.

But further promise is present—protection and deliverance. God promises to break the curse that the Fall placed on every area of our lives. The word of the Lord through the prophet Malachi throws down the gauntlet specifically in front of people who claim God's covenant of salvation but who reject His covenant in matters of finance. He says they are "cursed with a curse." This is not the curse of eternal loss in hell, but the curse of temporal loss because they close the door on God's financial pact of blessing.

Let's get a clear picture of this. It is important.

We all understand that Jesus' death and resurrection took care of the threefold curse of man's Fall: the curse of sinning, sickness and poverty. When Jesus died on the cross, breaking the power of all that cursed us, His goal was to bring us out—completely out—from under "the curse" affecting every area of our lives. When we live under the full dimensions of His covenant, we are curse-free:

- *The covenant of salvation* removes the curse of the penalty of eternal death.[3]

- *The covenant of healing* brings the potential for special blessings of God's strength, nurturing, sustaining of health and healing of affliction.[4]

But there is more. Like these two covenants, His *covenant of provision*[5] breaks the curse of poverty and smites "the devourer" that wreaks havoc with our finances.

The foundation of these covenant truths is lodged in God's original intent for man, and the blessing that redemption now offers to reinstate.

When man fell, he lost his God-given place of rulership, the role that had placed him originally in dominion over all things, provided he walk humbly with God.[6]

Now, in Christ, God offers full redemption and restoration from the curse. He wants to reinstate us in a place of spiritual rulership, seating us with Him as joint-heirs;[7] to partner with Him as possessors of "all things."[8] (Note especially that 1 Timothy 6:17–19 makes clear that financial abundance is a blessing only when it is experienced in the spirit of unselfishness, service and giving.)

Within this arena of promise—the covenant of provision—the Lord says that we can choose to participate or not. But if we choose not to live in this covenant, we expose ourselves to the limits of a "cursed environment."[9]

This does not mean that God will pour a cauldron of evil on me. Neither does it mean that I will be damned if I do not tithe. But it does mean that the economic affairs of my life have been forfeited or abandoned to the best that earth can provide or I can gain; and that is awfully small compared to how God can bless. It is a sad prospect to have your financial life chained to the impact of the Fall, or to the limitations of your own ingenuity, health or abilities.

God's promise, then, as we obey the covenant of the tithe is that He will rebuke the devourer. (This is as true individually as it is corporately.) In that ancient agricultural society, "the devourer" was the locusts—the swarms of insects that came seasonally and stripped the fields. At times it was the excessive heat that brought famine and withered the crops, or the premature delivery of the cattle so that they lost their young, or the early dropping of the grapes from the vines so that no harvest could be garnered. These all "devoured" in that ancient day. Today the devourer manifests itself in different ways—a shortage of what you expected, a withering of what might have been, the unexpected repairs straining the budget, the door of opportunity slammed in your face, the medical bills eating up your income—but the Lord still promises, *I will rebuke the devourer.*

- He will remove you from fruitless enterprises.

- He will overthrow what consumes the fruit of your labor.

- He will squash what cripples your efforts at productivity.

But He says gently, "I can do that only when you live within My promise—when you come under the canopy of My covenant."

God longs to work His desire for our abundance as we learn how to manage resources and distribute them with an equally abundant spirit. He wants to extricate us from the poverty-mindedness of the world system and introduce us to the eternal principles of financial management.

> "Give, and it will be given to you: good measure, pressed down, shaken together, and running over will be put into your bosom. For with the same measure that you use, it will be measured back to you."
> Luke 6:38

This is no magic-wand principle. I reject wholly the popularized notion that to break poverty is to enter into a self-gratifying wealth. We do not tithe to "get" something from God. That is an unscriptural and counterproductive way of thinking that presumes we can arm-wrestle money, things, healings or actions from God. That kind of reasoning only gives way to a legalism of formula-faith; ritualized laws that produce a bondage to "works." But the Lord wants to bring us to a view of release, with Him as our Liberator.

Without recognizing it, some have proposed an unbiblical, humanistic theology of abundance that is nothing more than an attempt to justify North American acquisitiveness and affluence. This attempt to give license to selfishness dissolves in the face of life's realities lived by most people throughout the world. Neither will it hold water when character-testing trials confront believers in this land. Learning to give does not preempt recurrent lessons in faith or periodic confrontations with the fearful spirit of poverty. Paul rejoiced in the fact that he had learned "how to be abased, and . . . how to abound" (Philippians 4:12), with the understanding that times of prosperity and times of financial strain both contain valuable lessons of faith.

I affirm that God wants us to abound, in whatever circumstance we find ourselves, and that the Bible teaches that poverty is a broken curse. But the abundance He wants to lavish upon us—upon His Church—is not for our own aggrandizement. It is for our service and ministry to the rest of His Body and to the world.

And there is one more thing.

The breaking of poverty does not suggest a superficial justification of affluence, nor does it result from a mismanaged giveaway philosophy. Some idealists have proposed that everyone in the Church give away everything. They propose that if we are to be "like the New Testament Church, everybody should be equally well—or poorly—off." But the book of Acts does not teach that.

Acts 4:32–5:11 illustrates a responsible *sharing in need,* not an equalizing of resources. God blesses people who learn diligence, order and management, and no guilt should be associated with a person's abundance. The possession of "much" is not the key to freedom from poverty. The key is to be free from the need to get; free from the need to be in control; free from the need to protect ourselves compulsively at every turn; free to live openheartedly and openhandedly, in submission to God's ways concerning our relationships and possessions.

Our treatment of people or our money management should not become an enemy to our fruitfulness and durability in building our lives.

Build an eternal quality into your life now.

To live as a person of temporal means and circumstance is to live far outside the circle of God's intended purpose for us. He calls us to live in another dimension of life—the eternal dimension where the spirit of poverty is broken.

Living this way breaks the need to manipulate circumstances or relationships. It breaks the need to manage money by giving grudgingly rather than by giving generously.

To live in that dimension above the world allows us to introduce a constant flow of His life into the world. And that world needs unselfish, loving, serving, humble, faithful givers—people who have tasted the victory of poverty's defeat as God has taught them the way to triumph.

So it was that He began teaching the "giving way" to me. We began to realize the beginning of freedom from the yoke of poverty.

1. Monies tithed were discovered to "cost" us nothing; for God's blessing, which cannot be bought, is released through this obedience.

2. People released in faith to serve elsewhere went away with their relationship with us intact, and the Holy Spirit was freed to expand us because of our interest in Christ's whole Church, rather than a preoccupation with only our own.

Thus, people sent are given, not "lost." Monies sent are expended or directed or invested, not "spent." We never lose or spend what we receive from God's hand as a gift, and what we in turn give in His way by His Spirit. Dr. Bob Pierce, the founder of World Vision and a man who possessed an unselfish passion for a needy world, loved to quote from the Dutch translation of 1 Chronicles 29:14:

"All that we have comes from Him, and we simply give it to you from out of God's own hand."

Notes

1 Romans 4:12–16.
2 Genesis 14:20.
3 Romans 10:9–10.
4 Exodus 15:26.
5 Malachi 3:8–12.
6 Genesis 1:28–29; 2:15–17.
7 Romans 8:16–17; Ephesians 2:6.
8 1 Timothy 6:17–19.
9 Malachi 3:8–12.

11

When We Come Together

The flow of the church service is a significant factor in determining the release of a congregation's life and the individual's ministry. These gatherings can be fruitful or frustrating, and the difference is found in the *order*—the sequence, design and direction—of the meeting.

In the Corinthian church, we see an excellent case study of order being retrieved from chaos in one congregation's services. Since few congregations have problems of hyperactivity, we can study such a case profitably, for here is apostolic order, both 1) in making room for *ministry and participation* by the gathered assembly; and 2) in maintaining a *respectful and sensible order* in the tenor of their times together.

We will understand 1 Corinthians 14 best when we recognize that it spoke to a spiritually alive congregation that needed help conducting its gathering times. The various problems debated so often in this text are more readily resolved when we see that this young group of Spirit-filled believers was relatively new at worshiping and fellowshiping together.

Their careless spontaneity in expressing spiritual language; their failure to recognize priorities among spiritual gifts; their insensitivity to newcomers in their midst; their apparent inclination to gullibility where prophetic utterance was concerned; their problem with what seems to be an inappropriate takeover of leadership by women— all these difficulties were related to their "church services," as we would call them.

As chapter 14 unfolds, after spending considerable time instructing them in how to sort out the difference between (a) the private and devotional exercise of tongues from (b) the public and prophetic exercise of spiritual language, Paul poses this inquiry: "How is it then, brethren?" In other words, "How shall we now fit this all together?"

Then he answers his own question by urging broad involvement and the expression of multiple ministries of the Holy Spirit's gifts among the assembly. Yet he still restricts all ministry to only that which edifies:

> Whenever you come together, each of you has a psalm, has a teaching, has a tongue, has a revelation, has an interpretation. Let all things be done for edification.   1 Corinthians 14:26

This statement sets forth two principles:

1.   Different members of the assembly will have various things to bring; thus, a reasonable order must be observed.

2.   Everything that is brought should build up the assembled body; that is, contribute to the general benefit— not just a private agenda.

To this day, merging these principles is a challenging proposition. Even in a small congregation of thirty or forty believers, it is difficult to know how everyone can share with and edify those gathered without protracting the service.

Further, the sad track record is well-established. Allowing anyone or everyone to express himself anytime or any way, under the guise of "letting the Holy Spirit have His way," is seldom as edifying as it is disrupting, time-consuming or confusing! Thus, most of us who lead are called to plan services, hoping to find ways to make them efficient without sacrificing effectiveness.

The goal of strong, corporate worship and maturing, balanced teaching is paramount. But even if that is achieved in our services, when church is over I as pastor must ask myself this question: "Has each one of the body been expanded in *ministry,* or has there only been dissemination of knowledge?" Information needs to be integrated with life through application and interaction. How?

We have targeted our gatherings to minister to *the Lord, the saints* and *the world.* First, through singing, praise and receiving the Word, we pursue ministering to *Him;* worshiping at His throne, studying His Word is *that* "ministry." Second, we pursue interactive involvement with each person present. Fellowship before and after the service helps, but each believer must be more personally involved if he is to become equipped to fulfill his role as an agent of Jesus in life's marketplace.

True fellowship requires direct interaction. People will not grow in ministry with only a quick handshake during church and intellectual ideas from the pulpit. They must also encounter, talk, pray—express care and concern firsthand and learn practical patterns of responses for the kinds of needs they meet daily.

It is not enough simply to say, in effect, "Listen to the truth *here and now,* and see that you act on it *there and then.*" It will probably help more to say, "As you are hearing truth, tell it here. As we explain ministry, get started in doing it in some way now." So in every gathering we try to have some opportunity to apply the truth being taught to flesh-and-blood circumstances.

Training members for ministry takes more than annual seminars, weekend retreats or special series. If we can offer training *action* every time we meet, we will take great strides in mobilizing the membership. Thus, simply by developing the most available time we have—our regular church services—we can advance the development of ministry-mindedness.

If the words of the Corinthian text provide a guide for member ministry, we find these things to focus on while we are gathered as a congregation.

1. We want to become a congregation that gives place to the gifts of the Holy Spirit listed in 1 Corinthians 12:8–10 and elaborated on in chapters 13 and 14.

2. We want to become a congregation committed to the systematic and edifying teaching of the Word of God as suggested in 1 Corinthians 14:19–20.

3. We want to become a congregation devoted to the exercise of Holy Spirit-inspired worship, commended in 1 Corinthians 14:2, 14–17.

4.   We want to become a congregation in which every
        member is involved as much as possible, as recom-
        mended in 1 Corinthians 14:26.

Now, how can we arrange an orderly service with worship, personal participation, strong Bible teaching and
expression of the gifts of the Spirit, all in fewer than
ninety minutes? I will try to describe how we pursue this
in our services but, first, may I establish three control-
ling propositions that guide us?

1.   We attempt to conduct our gathering times on the
        basis of what we think we have found in God's Word.
        We are not trying merely to justify what we want to do
        with a proof text.

2.   We have different and distinct goals for each of the
        three primary public services that make up the weekly
        program, so a somewhat specific and different pattern
        is in effect for each one. We do, of course,
        expect the Holy Spirit to work creatively within
        each pattern, and we are more than willing to allow
        Him to alter our patterns. In other words, we "keep
        open."

3.   We also understand that people may feel uncomfort-
        able in a service that requires forthright participation.
        Accordingly, we prod people forward gently, but refuse
        to concede to the pressure or convenience of social cus-
        tom.

We are even willing to lose potential members if believers will not be open to their own growth potential.
That may sound heartless, but we have discovered this
resistance or reticence in participation is *not* character-

istic of the unconverted visitor, but only of the experienced Christian! Since mere attendance has been allowed to substitute for discipleship in so much of the Church, instructional on-the-spot ministry, personal participation in prayer and warm interaction in the services sometimes put off "well-oriented" churchgoers.

We have also established a reputation for balancing liberty and order. There is something about that fact that contributes to people's feeling free to participate. You may enjoy reading what guests at our services often do—a word of assurance that we rerun frequently in the bulletin.

You're Safe Here

At The Church On The Way, we have committed ourselves to biblical principles of life and love which, we trust, will constantly manifest in such a way as to ensure those present here of the following:

Our freedom in worship will never surrender to fanaticism.

We are forthright and expressive, but differentiate between the *sound of praise* and the *noise of people*. We worship as a choir in chorus, not as soloists in competition. We worship in spirit with liberty, but in concert under leadership. It's safe to praise aloud with us, for we will partner together to worship in the *beauty* of holiness, and we will preempt both prideful formalism and personal fanaticism.

Our openness to one another will never exploit anyone.

We foster communication and interaction, recognizing that true fellowship is impossible without the pursuit of transparent and authentic sharing. What is shared in prayer is sacred with us, and what is shown from your heart is treasured. We hold this trust, that all who minister the life of Jesus to one another always function in the love of Jesus. That love is unconditional and non-manipulative, and it always covers weakness and sin with strength and forgiveness.

Our welcome to spiritual gifts will never violate the Word.

We ask the Holy Spirit to be present here and to distribute gifts among us according to His will. All the gifts are present in the Church, and every believer is urged to be free and responsible to minister gifts with sensitivity. We are covetous of their manifestation, but not gullible as to their demonstration. Graciousness in ministry, submissiveness in spirit and order in operation of the gifts is scriptural and, therefore, insisted upon in this assembly.

Our joyousness will never degenerate to mere excitability.

Childlike simplicity and faith can transcend patterns of pomp and pride, which society dictates we accept. But child*like* is not child*ish*, and so we refuse to be bound to the idea that true simplicity is either glib or emotionalistic. The joy and release in laughter, applause, shouting or tears involve the emotions; but, for understood reasons, not merely sensational ones. True freedom is as thoughtful as it is liberated, and we choose to live in that freeing truth.

In all, our prayerful wish is to live as the Church manifested at her birth:

So continuing daily with one accord in the temple, and breaking bread from house to house, they ate their food with gladness and simplicity of heart, praising God and having favor with all the people. And the Lord added to the church daily those who were being saved.   Acts 2:46–47

Involvement and Balance

Paul wrote 1 Corinthians 14 to a band of disciples who were not hesitant to be involved! Many were former pagans who did not know how to "be quiet in church," and many were excessively exuberant and disorderly when they gathered. It is easy to criticize this active bunch, but an equal and opposite error befalls us today when we prefer merely to be spectators. At least the Corinthians were in no danger of that! They needed balance and wisdom, and God gave them apostolic instruction and correction with patience to keep their train on track. Let's read the Holy Spirit's counsel given them, and see what that teaching still reveals to us today.

Following is a freely phrased, concept-by-concept analysis of the text as we have come to understand it. Examine it thoughtfully. Compare it with your own formal translation of the Bible and see what you think. Having carefully studied the Word for years in the light of both—the biblical text and the chemistry of vital experience—I believe there are workable conclusions here. I think the Word has provided a biblical basis for the discreet conduct of lively, interactive church gatherings right here in New Testament terms.

A Functional Paraphrastic Analysis of
1 Corinthians 14

1. Pursue love, and desire spiritual gifts, but especially that you may prophesy.

Verse 1 ... Love is always paramount and spiritual gifts are desirable, but clear communication is essential when you gather.

2. For he who speaks in a tongue does not speak to men but to God, for no one understands him; however, in the spirit he speaks mysteries.
3. But he who prophesies speaks edification and exhortation and comfort to men.
4. He who speaks in a tongue edifies himself, but he who prophesies edifies the church.
5. I wish you all spoke with tongues, but even more that you prophesied; for he who prophesies is greater than he who speaks with tongues, unless indeed he interprets, that the church may receive edification.
6. But now, brethren, if I come to you speaking with tongues, what shall I profit you unless I speak to you either by revelation, by knowledge, by prophesying, or by teaching?
7. Even things without life, whether flute or harp, when they make a sound, unless they make a distinction in the sounds, how will it be known what is piped or played?

Verses 2–25 ... Speaking with tongues in public without interpretation is counterproductive. The chief benefits of *prayer* with tongues are: communication with God (v. 2); the edifying of your inner man (v. 4; see also Jude 20 and Ephesians 3:16–17); and prayer and worship beyond your intellectual resources (vv. 14–15, 17).

The indiscriminate exercise of tongues in public gatherings defeats your purpose in coming together (vv. 6–8). The purpose is for the *whole* church to be built up and edified (v. 5), which requires those present to understand and participate.

8. For if the trumpet makes an uncertain sound, who will prepare himself for battle?

9. So likewise you, unless you utter by the tongue words easy to understand, how will it be known what is spoken? For you will be speaking into the air.

10. There are, it may be, so many kinds of languages in the world, and none of them is without significance.

11. Therefore, if I do not know the meaning of the language, I shall be a foreigner to him who speaks, and he who speaks will be a foreigner to me.

12. Even so you, since you are zealous for spiritual gifts, let it be for the edification of the church that you seek to excel.

13. Therefore let him who speaks in a tongue pray that he may interpret.

14. For if I pray in a tongue, my spirit prays, but my understanding is unfruitful.

15. What is the result then? I will pray with the spirit, and I will also pray with the understanding. I will sing with the spirit, and I will also sing with the understanding.

16. Otherwise, if you bless with the spirit, how will he who occupies the place of the uninformed say "Amen" at your giving of thanks, since he does not understand what you say?

17. For you indeed give thanks well, but the other is not edified.

This edifying benefit cannot take place as it should (vv. 9, 11, 16) unless the congregation adheres to basic order (vv. 12–13).

Because of this instruction, no one should think any language he or she speaks is unimportant (v. 10). Still, "tongues" is one's *spirit* at prayer, and the human understanding does not grasp the meaning (v. 14). Therefore, distinguish between "spirit" prayer and song (in tongues) and "understandable" prayer and song (in your native language), and employ each at appropriate times beneficial to all (v. 15-17).

18. I thank my God I speak with tongues more than you all;

19. yet in the church I would rather speak five words with my understanding, that I may teach others also, than ten thousand words in a tongue.

20. Brethren, do not be children in understanding; however, in malice be babes, but in understanding be mature.

21. In the law it is written: *"With men of other tongues and other lips I will speak to this people; and yet, for all that, they will not hear Me,"* says the Lord.

22. Therefore tongues are for a sign, not to those who believe but to unbelievers; but prophesying is not for unbelievers but for those who believe.

23. Therefore if the whole church comes together in one place, and all speak with tongues, and there come in those who are uninformed or unbelievers, will they not say that you are out of your mind?

24. But if all prophesy, and an unbeliever or an uninformed person comes in, he is convinced by all, he is judged by all.

25. And thus the secrets of his heart are revealed; and so, falling down on his face, he will worship God and report that God is truly among you.

26. How is it then, brethren? Whenever you come together, each of you has a psalm, has a teaching, has a tongue, has a revelation, has an interpretation. Let all things be done for edification.

When you observe proper order in a childlike and mature spirit (v. 20), people will not think you insane (v. 23); but instead, many will be moved and won by the power of the Holy Spirit working in each of you (vv. 24–25).

I am not demeaning glossolalia (v. 18), but am setting an absolute priority and control upon the method of your communications when you assemble (v. 19).

Verses 26–40 ... Each of you should plan to come with something to share, but it *must* be worthwhile (vv. 26–31). If the public

27. If anyone speaks in a tongue, let there be two or at the most three, each in turn, and let one interpret.
28. But if there is no interpreter, let him keep silent in church, and let him speak to himself and to God.
29. Let two or three prophets speak, and let the others judge.
30. But if anything is revealed to another who sits by, let the first keep silent.
31. For you can all prophesy one by one, that all may learn and all may be encouraged.
32. And the spirits of the prophets are subject to the prophets.
33. For God is not the author of confusion but of peace, as in all the churches of the saints.
34. Let your women keep silent in the churches, for they are not permitted to speak; but they are to be submissive, as the law also says.
35. And if they want to learn something, let them ask their own husbands at home; for it is shameful for women to speak in church.
36. Or did the word of God come originally from you? Or was it you only that it reached?
37. If anyone thinks himself to be a prophet or spiritual, let him acknowledge that the things which I write to you are the commandments of the Lord.
38. But if anyone is ignorant, let him be ignorant.

gift of tongues (always with interpretation) or the gift of prophecy is exercised, the number of participants should be limited (vv. 27, 29). Those who are mature should be responsible to evaluate what is said (v. 29). This is no restraint upon the Holy Spirit, but Spirit-filled people should restrain themselves (vv. 28, 30, 32). God is consistently a God of orderliness, which brings peace when a congregation assembles (v. 33). In this regard, remember three things:

First, disallow women to converse indiscriminately during the gathering time: That can wait until they are home (vv. 34–35. Note: 1 Corinthians 11:5 makes it clear that women can and do participate. The issue here is contrasting appropriate with noncontributive comment.)

39. Therefore, brethren, desire earnestly to prophesy, and do not forbid to speak with tongues.
40. Let all things be done decently and in order.

Second, truly sensible and spiritual members will affirm the wisdom of what I am saying. If they don't, that is their problem (vv. 36–38).

Third, desire clear communication at all times, although that is no argument against the proper place of speaking with tongues (v. 39). Be certain that everything is done in a graciously compelling and decorous manner (Gk. *euschemonos*), and that a sensible sequence and timing are maintained (v. 40).

As cursory as this coverage may be, a more detailed examination of the text will bear the weight of the proposition that this passage certainly calls for orderly services. But "order" will *release* worship, *release* the flow of gifts and *release* ministry as the ministry-mindedness of everyone present is developed.

The Thrust of Services

As I said earlier, we have a distinct target for each gathering time in general, as well as for each service specifically. For whatever it may contribute to your thought and plan, let me describe ours.

Sunday Morning

On Sunday morning we gather to carry out the three-fold ministry that characterizes our mission as a congregation.

Worship: We exalt the name of Jesus Christ and summon every person to "enter into His gates with thanksgiving, and into His courts with praise" (Psalm 100:4). From the platform, we direct prayer, praise and other expressions of worship, but at the same time we try to give simple guidelines to encourage each person to express his own sensitive and thoughtful worship.

Beside meaning-filled choruses, we sing at least one historic hymn to anchor ourselves to the traditional testimony of the people of God throughout the centuries. Although this use of hymnody occupies fewer than five minutes, we believe this habit to be significant. By it we declare our commitment to sound doctrine, our respect for the past and our adherence to timeless truths as expressed in the Church.

Fellowship: "Ministrytime" is a service segment usually framed by a focus on the Word of God. Our small group interaction and prayer together (three to five in a circle) is not merely an exercise in humanistic goodwill; it is a whole lot more. First, we set ourselves to apply some truth from the Scriptures, giving depth and biblical purpose to our interaction. I will usually explain a text and suggest how to apply it as we "minister" to (that is, *share* with, *pray* with, *love* and *care* for) one another. Drawing everyone into the small circles of prayer and sharing is crucial, especially where the visitor is concerned. We do this graciously, and have found that drawing visitors into the circles makes them feel loved rather than offended. We are committed to "every member—every person—participating" and are constantly seeking creative ways to implement that practice.

In this regard, we use songs as part of the teaching flow of the service. Music helps us focus on the particular truth being emphasized. In my past I was exposed to services that seemed to select choruses arbitrarily. I have come to feel that that is fundamentally dishonest with God, and with the congregation. It is so much more profitable if what we speak and what we sing move constantly toward the goal of the gathering. This type of thoughtful planning and direction is at the heart of *order* in a service.

Many have considered themselves "led of the Holy Spirit" when a service drifts from theme to theme with no coherence. This is *not* usually Holy Spirit motivation but human subjectivity, and it is the cause for pointless gatherings and wearying, dragging-on-and-on services.

Another thing we seek to sustain is a sense of "we're all in this together." Whenever we assemble, everything we do is *corporate*. Our services are not a mass rally of people conducting their private or small group devotions. Rather, we are *together*, so let's *all* do what we are doing. Opening the service to random participation may seem democratic, but it takes careful thought and gracious leadership to include everyone. Let's all become that kind of leader. People will not feel manipulated if the leader's spirit is that of a servant. But being a servant-leader still requires *leading*, not following the whims of the crowd.

In a certain respect, Sunday morning is always Easter at our place! It is the weekly renewal of our celebrating the Lord's day—*the beginning of the new creation in Jesus Christ!* This is an affair of state in the Kingdom of God, so we let triumph key the service. This does not mean we bind ourselves with burdens of pompousness or ceremony, but it does mean we get to the point, do it jubilantly, avoid whatever wastes time or is a mere indulgence of fruitless habit.

Teaching: The teaching of the Word has a large part in this service. Sometimes I distribute prepared outlines, designed for both immediate use and later study, and other times display key points on the overhead screens. The focus of the study is on building believers. We seek both to *mend* and *equip* believers for ministry. People who are tempted, wounded, broken and distressed need to hear a word of hope. People who are eager to relate truth to life, and life to those around them, need to hear it, too. Thus, the message of the morning fulfills the target of the three-fold ministry:

1. Worship and song, prayer and praise is our ministry to the Lord.

2. Prayer and sharing, personal interaction is our ministry to the saints.

3. Teaching the truth and preparing for service equips us for our ministry to the world.

All of these interrelate, of course, and in any "dissection" of details it seems that something of the whole is sacrificed, but the basic components are there, as are the concepts we seek to serve in each Sunday morning service.

Sunday Evening

While our Sunday morning services follow a fairly consistent pattern, our evening gatherings vary widely in their thrust and application. We always seek, however, to retain the common denominator of a sustained warmth and growth together as a "family"—a body growing and enjoying life in Jesus.

Expositional studies of the Bible and special series elucidate practical biblical themes. Musical programs celebrate biblical truths or holidays. Guests or staff speakers address important aspects of life.

Segments like these constitute the larger part of a given Sunday evening meeting. An opening time of worship is followed by water baptism; and, aside from the principal presentation mentioned above, little else is planned.

Worship and praise are bright with promise and alive with freshness. Some gifted member may sing or a group may present music, dance or instrumental messages, but the primary focus is *straight Bible.*

In any service, however, at any time in the week, what is planned never preempts what may be perceived as a need for adjusting the plan. A song may ignite an especially unusual response, and we will give place to the flow of that work of God's grace; or we may invite testimonies or a report of some recent event in which God's power was at work; or someone in the congregation may have a word of prophecy or a timely exhortation.

Giving *a* place to spontaneous expressions, however, does not require that leaders give *the* place to it. In other words, because something is allowed does not mean that "anything goes." Nor does an alteration in the service plan mean that the whole plan is scrapped. Beautiful innovations and divine interruptions are welcome, but because, as leaders, we approach our gatherings with considerable prayer and preparation, we seem generally to have the mind of the Lord for the basic direction of that service. I hasten to add, however: We choose always to expect something unexpected. We believe the Holy Spirit will do *something* special—a divine, lovely and distinctive surprise of some kind—in virtually every service.

Perhaps it will also help to describe how we respond to the gifts of the Holy Spirit in the public services. First, we *expect* gifts to be manifested—to flow among all the members of the body (see 1 Corinthians 12); and, second, we maintain order in their exercise (see 1 Corinthians 14). With those as axiomatic, how then do we proceed?

Two biblical guidelines serve our congregation well in this regard.

First, since "the spirit of the prophet is subject to the prophet" (1 Corinthians 14:32), we do not believe a gift must of necessity "burst forth" uncontrollably. The individual who feels that the Holy Spirit has prompted him or her to prophesy, speak in a tongue, interpret or exercise some other gift is generally required to indicate this to someone leading the service. There are some more spontaneous exercises of vocal gifts, however, and this is not generally discouraged. I recently wrote a brief article on this subject for *Ministries Today* magazine describing this aspect of ministry by seeking to answer a pastor's

question: "How should public 'prophecy' be regulated?"
This article follows:

Despise Not Prophesying

How do you handle "prophecies" given to you or spoken to your flock?

I've had situations tempt me to despise prophecies, haven't you? How many lives have been shredded by misguided or manipulative "words from the Lord"; how many church services divided by a veil of confusion—all because of a prophetic "word"? No wonder Paul had to warn against "despising" prophesying.

Harper's *Lexicon* defines *exoutheneo* (despise) as "to make light of, to set at naught, to treat or reject with scorn." In short, I am not to *mock, deride* or *cheapen* the place of prophecy.

In this sense, prophecy is a means by which several members may participate in a service, prompted by the Holy Spirit to relate ideas or thoughts—"a word"—which may edify, exhort or comfort. It is *a* word, always to be based upon and measured by *the* Word.

As a pastor, I need to

- *deliver* prophetic "words" God gives me,

- *respond* to those "words" ministered from the assembly, and

- *integrate* vital "words" into the body life.

How can I release this gift's blessing without confusion?

I was speaking to a gathering of churches in one city recently when suddenly a prophecy boomed forth. I listened carefully, first, to hear the content; second, to sense the mixed crowd—many of whom were unaccustomed to such utterances. The ill-conceived "word" absolutely quenched the strong spirit of prayer upon the group.

Looking around, I winced in noting the man who was sounding forth as the "voice of God." I not only knew him (a sincere soul), but years ago I was his pastor. I remember the delicate line I sought to walk, trying to help release his gifting and teach him balance and discipline in its exercise. He clearly had forgotten those lessons, and though the meeting wasn't ruined, it wasn't helped.

I went to him later asking why he hadn't first submitted the word to the leaders of the meeting. He bluntly replied, "I did what the Lord told me to do!"

Had he? I don't think so.

1 Corinthians 14:26–40 gives clear instruction on how the Spirit's gift of prophecy can be ministered *and* administered. The teaching is that a prophecy (i.e., a truth God wants to remind us about or encourage us with) is to be judged. This means to evaluate it—to weigh what has been said in the light of the Bible's teaching, and to determine the place into which the message fits in the flow of a service. It also includes application: what ought to be done in response to the insight the "word" brings. (I lament the glib habit of applauding prophetic words as though the whole idea of the gift were to excite us.)

In my early ministry, I was uncertain how to welcome prophesying without inviting problems. Then I was introduced to the concept of "submitting the word." By submitting, I mean that anyone feeling God has given him or her a "word" *first* present the gist of the message to an elder. I believe this is as valid a fulfillment of the apostolic directive to judge the prophecy as if we waited until it were given publicly.

At first I wondered if this practice might obstruct the liberty of the Spirit, but instead I found it *released* ministry. Individuals sensing the Spirit's prompting with a word were liberated, and the congregation seemed freer to receive. This custom removed the person's appearing to be seizing the service at his own discretion. Members of the body learn to trust eldership who assist the release of the gifting within the assembly. Thus, when during a worship segment of the service a member submits a word to an elder, our goal is to see that that word ministers, not to repress it in a hierarchical manner.

At times a submitted prophecy is given almost immediately; another time it will be reserved until later in the service. On occasion the person submitting a word will be asked simply to receive the word as for himself, not the body, or to reserve the word for another occasion, as it doesn't seem to synchronize with this gathering.

In all, such steps seem to help avoid "despising" and assist "releasing" and being edified.

* * *

That article met with a generally favorable response, but a few protests. That isn't surprising, for some fear that order will crush liberty, while in fact the opposite is true. Graciously administered order *keeps* the freedom for the Holy Spirit to minister to and through the *whole* body, rather than being commandeered and controlled by one or two.

I suppose we always risk hurting someone's feelings by

requiring order in this way, but this seems the best path of balance between two entirely undesirable courses: either (1) giving no place at all to the Spirit's working, or (2) exercising no control whatever.

As years have passed, any fears of quenching the Spirit have proven unjustified. We still experience the ongoing ministry of the Holy Spirit to our congregation through words of prophecy, exhortation, wisdom and knowledge, even though the size of the congregation makes it a little more difficult to administer and somewhat more intimidating for the average person to address the whole assembly. Small groups allow a sufficient arena for "all to prophesy," however, and anyone who wants to submit a word for the whole body by writing our pastoral offices knows he or she is welcome to do so.

Prayer Meeting

This is our third service of the week. It is so powerful, joyous and buoyant that it deserves a chapter of its own, for God has taught us some of our weightiest and mightiest lessons at our midweek gatherings.

12

The Fellowship and the "Firepower"

The words *prayer meeting* tend to conjure images of a small group of musty people gathering for superstitious reasons, mumbling heavenward, and then dissolving quietly into the night. For many the idea carries all the mystique of a scene from *Wuthering Heights,* or the banality of contrived religiosity.

Not so here! At midweek service, the church rises in triumph to do its principal work in God's Kingdom. We move into blessed fellowship and powerful unity through worship, and then come to the primary purpose of our gathering: intercession and spiritual warfare.

If Sunday morning is "an affair of state" in the Kingdom, prayer meeting is "congress in session" or "army on the march." It starts with praise, advances with intercession and climaxes with teaching. The foundation for such an advance is the rich sense of community among us—something that has come about as our "ministry to the saints" (fellowship) has been joined to our ongoing commitment to "ministry to the Lord" (worship).

Prayer meeting is a dynamic demonstration of prayer's

"firepower" and of the way the army of God advances His Kingdom. Before we examine the explosive power of intercessory prayer, perhaps it would be best to look into the basis for unity among the troops.

Ministry to the Saints

The Bible, quite frankly, calls imperfect people "saints." Their holiness is fully established and secured, not through their own righteousness but through Christ's—purchased and provided for time and eternity by His cross. Thus, as partners in this forgiven and justified state with which God's grace has ennobled them, saints are called to edify, encourage, care for and love one another as "family"—as redeemed fellow citizens of God's Kingdom.

These are the grounds and the gist of fellowship: being loved by God and learning to love one another. And as I struggled with worship's priority, I found it nearly as hard to prioritize fellowship before evangelism in the Church's "ministry order." Worship, I could at least reason, is for God. But fellowship? That is only for *people;* in fact, it is for "already saved" people. It sure could seem selfish . . . I mean, if this *also* preceded the importance of evangelism. And furthermore, to my mind, "fellowship" smacked of church hall dinners with calorie-laden casseroles and superficial conversation; of people trying to act or sound adequately pious to qualify for acceptance among other Christians.

But this struggle with relative priority was soon laid to rest. First, because I realized that evangelism's importance was never in question when establishing these priorities. The issue was *sequence,* not importance: It all had to do with our perspective on the *path* and *process* of evangelism, and not which one seemed more important. It also involved redefining the purpose and practice of both worship and evangelism. Just as I had found new dimensions of worship, I knew there had to be something more in the New Testament idea of *koinonia.* The "fellowship" I had dismissed as unnecessary was not the original idea at all. Instead, true *koinonia,* I learned, is an ideal that begins to knit the Body of Christ together when three things take place: (1) clear definition, (2) the right atmosphere and (3) honest people.

In the New Testament, *fellowship* means "to share in common." The early Church *shared meals* together (Acts 2:46), *faced crises* together (Acts 4:23–24), *shared their resources* to meet one another's practical needs (Acts 4:34; 6:1) and *met together,* often in their homes (Acts 5:42). They were *growing together* under strong, steadfast teaching (Acts 2:42), and learning to *pray together,* like a football team being given the plays for use against their opponent.

The epistles are filled with references to fellowship in the many "one-to-another" verses they command. At every point of relationship, believers are called to love one another, care for one another, show concern for one another, pray for one another, serve one another, help one another or just plain be patient with one another. In this spirit, their lives become "locked in"—synchronized with one another. And soon, what becomes as impressive as it is amazing, this intimacy, transparency and unselfishness in fellowship—in the sustained atmosphere of regular and praiseful worship—seems to attract the rest of society. Look what happened amid worship and fellowship in the young Church:

> Now all who believed were together, and had all things in common, and sold their possessions and goods, and divided them among all, as anyone had need. So continuing daily with one accord in the temple, and breaking bread from house to house, they ate their food with gladness and simplicity of heart, praising God and having favor with all the people. And the Lord added to the church daily those who were being saved. Acts 2:44–47

Daily! People being saved every day—almost falling like overripe fruit into the hands of neighboring believers whose worship was warm and whose fellowship was real.

Let any of us who would evangelize ask ourselves, "How many people in our world long for genuine evidence that someone simply cares about them? How many—deep inside—hold the hope, the dream that sometime, somewhere, there could be a community of people who would do *both*—love God and love one another, purely, genuinely and steadfastly?" The answer is probably seen in this text. When the members of that fledgling church expressed their concern by caring and by sharing one another's needs, onlookers were drawn to them, caught somehow in what John Hurston calls "the web of love."

Ministry to the saints is neither more nor less than an openhearted and openhanded availability to love, share, help and care for each other. And it stuns the outsider to an awareness that self-giving relationships are possible in this world without several swigs of alcohol first or the promise of a "bedding" later.

Fullhearted worship and openhearted fellowship do not just happen. They spring from an atmosphere of understanding and trust. This atmosphere can really grow only where people understand God aright, and where their leaders are willing to model a basic transparency.

Let's look at these requirements.

Understanding God Aright

God, I had learned as a youth, is holy and just. Not as clear to me were His fatherly graciousness and mercy. It was not that no one had spoken of these truths concerning the Almighty; perhaps I had been partially blinded by my own idealism. I have come to realize that most of us feel inclined to accept condemnation as if it were a required, if not holy, emotion, something essential to prompt us forward on a quest for genuine holiness.

It was my years of ministry, the study and preparation beforehand and time spent teaching at LIFE Bible College that laid solid foundations in truth—practical, liberating truth upon which a life and a ministry could be built. I was taught of God's sovereign love and gift in Jesus, and of the solidarity of the believer's position before the Father through Christ's justifying work on the cross. I found the deep, securing peace that begets a true sense of personal identity, that identity gained when we learn to identify with Christ Himself. And I gained deliverance from the specter of condemnation.

It is a happy day to find out how *total forgiveness* is *totally provided;* how God's Word reveals that our *abso-*

lute acquittal from sin's record and judgment has been secured conclusively through the cross of Jesus. When the confidence born of these truths rises, a certainty of growth and of ultimate victory over one's own carnality becomes credible—and a genuine potential for joyous living opens up. In this climate, through the Holy Spirit's resurrection power flowing into every believer who begins to rest "in Christ," growth in love and strength in life increase as His full, promised provisions for us begin to be appropriated.

These basic points of biblical doctrine not only are anchoring, setting the soul in a high view of God's holiness and justice, but beget the context in which an atmosphere for true *koinonia* can be cultivated and taught to others— a fellowship based on "that which we have seen and heard" (see 1 John 1:3).

Here is where the crucial difference between "fellowship" as fostered in humanistic circles and *koinonia* as generated by the Holy Spirit is most easily seen. Mere camaraderie is the most a humanistic or "clannish" fellowship can produce. It is the warmth of a recovery group, the academic acceptance of a guild, a hearing-heart-and-ear at a bar, a bosom-buddy trust. It isn't that there are no redeeming features in such relationships, but simply that they have not the power to be redeeming *enough!* Even in the church, a "nice, happy feeling" or a sanctified glad-handism will not make it. While we might commend anything that urges a person to "be as much as you can, as noble as possible," this can never become truly redemptive.

Friendly, kind, generous—yes, perhaps, maybe.

But redemptively transforming, purely unconditional, dynamically comforting? Seldom, if ever, without God.

This path toward true fellowship also confronts a problem inherent in a merely social relationship. A spiritual, scripturally based *koinonia* cannot be indifferent to sin. Some see such a fellowship of understanding in the dim light of a philosophy based on "cheap grace"—a supposed spirituality sold as a generosity between brothers and sisters who "accept everyone unconditionally." All the words are right, but too much is lacking. Fellowship, like worship, is to exist in the light of the Lord's presence—in spirit and in truth. As the Word becomes incarnate in our lives, and as we speak its truth to each other in love, we will accept and encourage each other patiently, but we must confront anything that shadows the light. Otherwise there is no dynamic to lift any of us beyond where we are.

- True fellowship shares lifegiving power as well as tenderhearted understanding (Galatians 6:1–2).

- True fellowship is transparent and trusting; and by walking in the light of that fellowship, lives will be cleansed from bondage and disobedience (1 John 1:7).

- True fellowship accepts people where they are, but loves them forward and upward (John 8:11).

Our fellowship may indeed be an acknowledged "union of casualties" in the struggles and failures of life—a band of sinners en route to holiness. But true *koinonia* results in *progress,* and it begets growth and moves in victory; and it will foster graciousness, patience and understanding with those whose growth and victories seem slow in coming about.

It is delicate territory, walking the line of truth's balance between humanistic theory and legalistic theology. On the side of humanism, grace can be exaggerated in the name of gentleness and understanding, while on the side of legalism, biblical injunctions can be made into nails that seal the coffin of the wounded, burying them alive with a devastating sense of their own failure. We want to answer the challenge of finding that place between these two half-truths—a place where people can learn to fellowship in a full understanding of God's high call to obedience while still holding to an equal understanding of His merciful ways of patience, longsuffering and lovingkindness. The balance we sought at The Church On The Way called us to learn how to teach it and learn how to live in it.

The main thing I had to do was begin to trust myself to proclaim God's love with the ever-deepening conviction I was gaining about His desire *toward* and overwhelming commitment *to* all of us. I was nervous about some of my pastoral peers thinking I had turned loose and shallow. But I knew that my convictions were on a solid biblical and theological base, and that from those footings those being taught to rest in God's love and Christ's mighty work would grow solidly. And I was sure something else would grow: a ministry to the saints—a true, loving, accepting, forgiving fellowship among the Lord's people.

Now, as I committed to pastoring a people in this light and toward this three-pronged goal of sequenced priority—worship, fellowship and then evangelism—I found that the truths I have just related began to develop a new dynamism.

It was far easier to lead people in praise and worship of a God they knew to be compassionate. We were living in the pathway of worship according to the Word, which calls forth worship on the basis of God's graciousness. Such passages as Psalms 29, 96 and 136 and 2 Chronicles 20:21 guided us—all of them finding expression in our common exhortation to "praise the Lord in the beauty of holiness, for his mercy endureth forever."

I had been inclined to suppose that accomplished holiness was a prerequisite to "deep" worship. Now a clearer view was coming through God's revelation, which says, in effect, "In My sight you *are* beautifully holy. Praise Me for both what I have done to save you, and what I see you to be in Christ, even as you are becoming that. Thus, your worship shall be the pathway unto your further transformation into the likeness of My Son. And always remember: All the while *that* is happening, My mercy will last long enough to see you along the way!" Here is a place where anyone who *loves* the Lord can *enjoy* and *worship* Him in confidence and assurance. That is deep worship that builds truly deep people.

Transparent Leadership

With a freer devotion in worship taking hold, we were at the same time gaining an atmosphere of trust throughout the congregation. It grew as the leadership of the church learned to manifest transparency—an openness about our own lives and process of growth.

We were already finding that true *koinonia* could thrive in a climate in which genuine love flowed from the people and in which the people were discovering God's unending mercy and working toward constant obedience. Now this *koinonia* was beginning to liberate my own willingness for self-disclosure in preaching.

Because I believe in God's patience with me, a child seeking honestly to grow up in His will, I became bolder in sensitively (and tastefully) sharing some of my own stumblings and failures as I sought to follow Jesus. Episodes from my own struggles with growth and faith became a regular part of my teaching illustrations with the congregation. My preaching was still Word-centered, but it became far more applicable to life, as it was punctuated with cases of my own slowness to learn, inability to understand, stupidness toward sinning or impatient presumption.

As I learned to understand or laugh at myself, and tell about it, the congregation began to open up, too. We could accept each other all the more, because we were learning the practicality of living in the open light of a transparent walk with God. Bill Gaither's lyric says it with reference to God: "The One who knows me best loves me most." The same thing works among God's kids.

Our people could now share openly about their needs or areas of conflict, because the pastor himself was showing the way. Each of us began to realize that it can be "safe" to acknowledge our own weakness and need. Yet this atmosphere of acceptance was kept balanced, as each person's acknowledged need was joined to each person's commitment to allow the sanctifying grace of the Holy Spirit to bring him or her into Christ's character and likeness.

This order of fellowship is based on more than syrupy platitudes of acceptance or generalized good will. Such a spirit of trust and transparency is born of solid theology. Because our sovereign God has announced our acceptance in Christ, because the Almighty One has disclosed His patience with our slow growth out of weakness into His strength, therefore we can look up and live. With our heads held high in praise to Him, it is easier to turn and look into one another's eyes in open fellowship.

This kind of church body will become bold in faith and spiritual warfare, too. Just as with their salvation, so it is with their conflicts: They have learned that "the battle is not yours, but God's."[1]

From Fellowship to "Firepower"

The concept of spiritual warfare has been debated for centuries. Is it social? Intellectual? Physical? Political? Or "just" spiritual? The most constant arguments today seem to be over the theology of prayer warfare. This is too bad, because while some argue over whether or not it is right, their questions have not removed the reality of the struggle, but have only confused some of the troops.

Some teachers seem to feel that to suggest that a battle exists in which a praying Church makes a determinative difference is to reduce Jesus' victory on the cross, somehow to move redeemed man into a quasi-mediatorial role as a partial redeemer of mankind. Of course, nothing could be further from the position of those of us who hold to the biblical facts:

1. There is a battle (Ephesians 6:10–20);

2. The Church has been assigned a place of spiritual mission in prayer warfare (Romans 8:26–28, 16:20; 1 Timothy 2:1–4); and

3. The grounds for expected victory are solely and entirely in the established triumph of Christ's cross (Matthew 16:19, 18:18; Colossians 2:14–15).[2]

When the Church moves into prayer, she is actually drawing on the "firepower" of the cross. This is the only power that can break the *current* works of darkness, just as it is the only power that can break hell's hold on mankind. Prayer warfare confronts present satanic strongholds and prepares for the advance of the Gospel. (See Paul's request for the prayers of the Ephesians [6:19–20], so that dark strongholds could be broken open and the ministry of the Gospel could be forwarded.)

This whole idea of attack, battle and ongoing struggle against the works of hell is Jesus' idea. He knew what His achievement at Calvary would accomplish. He also knew that extending the dimensions of His dominion would be an age-long process. So He sought to infuse His disciples with understanding on this subject. He began this when He introduced a new word to them: *church.*

The concept of *church* was well-established before the time of Christ. The Greek word that we translate "church" is *ekklesia.* Its basic definition means "the called-out ones," and it found new importance in the vocabulary of ancient Greeks when the great city-states were being founded. The *ekklesia* did not mean a *place;* it referred to the *people,* the assemblies of citizens, and centered on their potential as a governing entity.

In fact, the primitive forms of *ekklesia* were employed in Greece when democracy was first being learned. The citizens convened to decide the issues that concerned them. They had until then depended upon (or had no choice but to accept) the unilateral decisions and actions of the king. But now the government was being entrusted to them, and their deliberations were determinative. They were the *ekklesia,* the assembly. Whatever was at issue—what tax should be levied, what law should apply, what war should be waged—the *ekklesia* was responsible to exercise the application of the power of the state.

Jesus adopted this meaning to underscore His Church's power for change, inherent in the people's application of power He was to entrust to them.

The Church at Prayer

This is the idea so fundamental to our approach to prayer warfare, to intercession. The concept is established on biblical premises, not upon Greek history. It centers in passages like Matthew 16:18–19, which guides our thinking like this:

1. All of God's power is vested in Christ, but it is the Father's will that those redeemed through His Son grow in redemptive partnership with Him.

2. Jesus has bequeathed His power for the mission of recovering earth to His Church, as the Holy Spirit exercises Christ's authority through the redeemed citizens of the Kingdom of God.

3. These citizens have been given the keys of the Kingdom—the right to apply His rule to circumstances they are authorized to encounter in His name.

4. Jesus said that if His Church would function in agreement and in the resources He has given her, "the gates of hell [the power and evil government of dark rulers in the invisible realm] will not be able to prevail [that is, sustain their hold on the ground they have taken]."

5. What Christ accomplished in the invisible realm through the cross (that's unconditional: "It is fin-

ished") now awaits application and advancement in the visible realm through the Church's obedience (that's conditional: Will she "occupy" until He comes?).

6. This condition is answered, of course, by the Church's witness in proclaiming the Gospel. But the Word clearly predicates the prospect of success in *all* proclamation and extension of the Gospel upon the spiritual dynamism of prayer (for example, 1 Corinthians 16:9; 2 Corinthians 10:3–6).

7. Further, the Church's intercession will be determinative in deciding the prevailing atmosphere of the evil society in which the people live (1 Timothy 2:1–3; 2 Chronicles 7:14).

8. Notice, prayer and spiritual action are the Church's promised resources for power, *not* political contacts or military might (2 Corinthians 10:4–5; Ephesians 6:10–12).

Perhaps those ideas will help us see the force and priority of Jesus' words when He declared His intent to build His Church.

A Look at Matthew 16:19

Allow me to take you on a phrase-by-phrase investigation of Jesus' commissioning words on the *ekklesia*'s methods of exercising the government He was planning to give them. Look at Matthew 16:19, which immediately follows His words "I will build My Church, and the gates of Hades shall not prevail against it"; that is, shall not be able to withstand its advance. Here's why:

Whatever you bind on earth:
"Whatever you may at any time bind (that is, establish, or apply the cross' contract concerning hell's power, or seek to stave off some satanic advance on earth);

Will be bound in heaven:
"has already been accomplished authoritatively in the spiritual realm, where the real contest takes place, by the power of My cross, resurrection and ascension to the seat of all power;

Whatever you loose on earth:
"And further, whatever (and only whenever) you may at any given point 'release, unlock or forgive' concerning any situation or person on earth;

Will be loosed in heaven:
"I have already secured the authority for that action in the realm of spiritual struggle through the cross and My resurrection."

This amplification and paraphrase is derived from the explicit meaning based on the moods, tense and voice employed in the Greek verbs so precisely used in this classic passage. When Jesus announced His plan to build His Church, He unfolded immediately the authority He was assigning to that people ("keys of the Kingdom") and the promise that hell will have to yield *if and when* (subjunctive mood, Greek) the Church applies that power of His victory.

This is no cheap or easy idea to embrace.

Sadly, the phrase *the authority of the believer* has become a slogan, almost a clever catchall for easy believism that seems to have been popularized in some segments of the renewed Church today. Take the slogan, for example, *What you say is what you get.* The problem is not the glibness in the words, but that the truth it represents cannot be rejected out-of-hand.

The Bible *does* recommend discreet, faith-filled speech. Indeed, personal salvation *begins* with it!

> If you confess with your mouth the Lord Jesus and believe in your heart that God has raised Him from the dead, you will be saved. For with the heart one believes to righteousness, and with the mouth confession is made to salvation.　　　Romans 10:9–10

And it is also true that lips of clay *can* dissolve the potential for realizing or receiving God's provisions because of one's exercising sloppy, unbelieving and spiritually scrambled speech.[3]

Our corporate action in spiritual warfare and authoritative prayer is not based on shallow humanism or parroted slogans. We have accepted God's summons to bold belief on biblical terms that build character, and our prayer meeting has become a continual, mighty, week-after-week act of faith. On the foundation of the victory of the cross, we march with a steadfastness of commitment to ceaseless intercession.

We have also added the biblical discipline of fasting as a means of intercession. Fasting is an instrument of spiritual conflict, and its force invigorates prayer. It is a discipline that Jesus applied (Matthew 4:2), taught (Matthew 17:21; Mark 9:29) and prophesied would continue among His people (Matthew 9:15; Luke 5:35), that the disciples accepted (Acts 13:2–3; 14:23) and that still works today. As we extend Calvary's claim of victory to people and nations in prayer, we do not always expect quick answers or easy victories. As we pray with fasting we do not suppose we are *earning* victory, but are *learning* a path of conquest over the enemy. Sure, there are setbacks and stalemates at times, but we will not give up. (See Jesus' teaching in Luke 18:1–8.)

As a congregation we seize grand issues in prayer—the government of nations, righteousness in lawmaking, the extension of the Gospel through barricades of adversity. But that does not keep us from "homey" issues. We are equally concerned and at prayer for a brother or sister who needs a job; a junior-high-schooler facing an examination; a man who needs healing from a heart condition; a loved one entering surgery next Monday; a drunken neighbor who has left his wife and kids; a motorcycle accident victim facing amputation; a family that has split up; a woman diagnosed with cancer.

Long-range universal and cosmopolitan issues interweave with immediate personal problems and human dilemmas. They are one and the same. We approach both on the basis of our right to invade these issues in prayer, expecting that God's will shall be done in the *here and now,* on earth, as it has already been established *then and there,* at the cross.[4]

Such is the tenor of this midweek meeting. To understand how this came about, it might help to travel quickly through the years of growth, experience, trial and slow learning we experienced. The spirit of intercession, a dynamic prayer meeting and a sense of divine destiny do not arrive overnight; nor will they continue without periodic renewals in faith, commitment and spiritual stamina.

The Beginnings

Few things are more depressing than a dead prayer meeting! A church's power base, shorn of its life, becomes the Church's most monstrous tradition.

When we first came, I set about making the prayer meeting exactly that—a *prayer* meeting. Some congregations opt for other midweek emphases: Bible studies, family nights, "total church action" nights—everything from prayer to choir practice. I have no judgment against any of these, but I was convinced that the Holy Spirit was calling us to become a people of prayer power.[5] Our Wednesday prayer meeting would be our laboratory to research the Church's power potential. So early on, I announced to our little flock (even "littler" on Wednesdays!) that we were going to pray *specifically, in faith,* and that we would *not get bogged down* in guessing games about requests and answers. This was illustrated with practical meaning one evening soon after I made the above qualifications.

One Wednesday, within weeks of my arrival, at the time prayer requests were invited, someone suggested, "Let's pray about the earthquake in Central America." One of the Latin American republics had been devastated, and it was unquestionably a worthy request. But it was the kind of request that is so often prayed over with vagueness, where no specifics are prayed so no answers are noticed. This "vagueness" usually derives from a sense of helplessness mixed with feelings of compassion, guilt and fear. Compassion derives from the need and pain the situation contains. Less perceived, yet often present, is guilt—feelings evoked because others are suffering and we are not. Fear is subtly present, too: "What if that had happened *here?*" But even if neither guilt nor fear is present, vagueness too often remains.

Though this sort of "Pray for the earthquake victims" request may sound thoughtful, it is very vulnerable to an unholy irresponsibility. It can seem—or actually be—the seeking of prayer as an escape from duty, somehow to dispense with the matter by throwing it at heaven. Words can be cast skyward without a genuine exercise of faith or a follow-through with action. Frankly, if prayer can be used this ignorantly in so apparently sincere a way, little power will be available to sustain the Church's life, because vital, faith-filled, sensible, action-ready prayer is the only real, living breath of the Church.

"That's good," I said to the person who had suggested we pray concerning the earthquake. "That disaster deserves prayer, and the Word of God holds real promise if we do pray. So, how shall we pray about the earthquake?"

Everyone looked at me blankly, dumbfounded by the follow-up question. Such matters, we had all believed, were simply "put into the hands of the Lord." This was time for another "Your will be done" in the face of hellishness. We supposed that once we had prayed, God would be responsible for whatever might happen now that nature had exploded.

"I don't want to be difficult," I continued, "but I think we should decide exactly how we are going to pray. It's too easy to speak a few words and leave the matter, since we've fulfilled our duty to mention it to the Almighty—as though He weren't aware of it. But our praying is able to accomplish a good deal more than simply taking note of the problem with compassion. I believe the Lord wants us to learn something through this request."

Then I asked another pointed question.

"First of all, let's decide: Did God *will* the earthquake? We need to think about this if we're going to ask Him to do anything there. Perhaps we don't know the full answer, but we do know this. Our broken-crusted earth, which slides and trembles as much as it does, is not quite the same planet God created and called 'good.' Man's Fall has fouled the planet as well as his own nature. The apostle Paul tells us in Romans 8 that the Fall subjected creation to things outside its originally intended order.[6] So, I'm proposing that God doesn't want earthquakes, and that He probably didn't 'will' this one.

"However," I continued, "at the same time, we can probably agree it didn't surprise Him, either. So with a solid sense that He knew in advance, He knows now and He wants things different from the way they are (those things impacted by the Fall), let's ask the Holy Spirit to show us how to pray about this disaster."

Everyone agreed, and we prayed to ask the Holy Spirit to do exactly that. Then we began to interact over the next few minutes, and we arrived at these requests which I wrote on the chalkboard.[7]

1. Pray for the bereaved, that the Spirit of God would comfort them.

2. Pray against bitterness finding an entrenched place in hearts that would blame God for the earthquake.

3. Pray for Gospel workers and believers to demonstrate the love, power and life of Jesus unto the salvation of souls.

4. Pray for rescue workers and relief agencies, that their efforts would be enabled by God's blessing and international help.

5. Pray that our interest would not recede following this prayer time, but that we would continue to pray, and that God would show us how to help in addition to praying.

Can you imagine what happened? The people prayed fervently, with faith and conviction. They sought God earnestly, that His hand be extended into this disastrous situation and that His love and peace be demonstrated. Later they watched the papers and other media for evidence of answers. At the same time, we decided to receive an offering to send to an appropriate relief agency; and, as it turned out, our own denomination became engrossed immediately in such relief through our missionary work there.

Many months later, the Foursquare missionary from that nation visited our congregation and told us what happened following the earthquake, since he knew of our interest through the gift we had sent. We were all thrilled to hear him recite specific matters of record that revealed God's hand moving along the exact lines we had prayed about!

That handling of the earthquake request established a basic stance.

A new mood began to govern our praying. We no longer just prayed. Instead we *defined* our objectives in prayer, *believed* our God would answer and *served* the situation in any way we could when that was possible. We also dispensed with the traditional appeal for unspoken requests. If something is to be prayed about, then it should be spoken. Occasionally matters must be described with discretion because of a confidence, a security issue or because of the intimacy involved. But this is not the usual case. The unspoken request idea has become terribly worn in our circles and deserves to be terminated. Further, generalized requests were stopped, like praying for "the missionaries" or praying for "all our unsaved loved ones." Now, when we pray we name missionaries, we name unsaved loved ones and we bring specific people and cases by name (usually first names only) before the throne of God.

We all probably need to overcome dishonest or lazy habits in our private prayer times or our prayer meetings. We sought new and living ways to show that when we prayed, we meant it.

And God heard and answered!

I am sorry now that we failed to keep a written record of answered prayer. Calls come every week from around the nation and the world, asking this congregation to pray. This is not to our credit, nor do I write these words to commend my own congregation. We are unworthy servants: We have done only what was our duty (Luke 17:10). That biblical viewpoint certainly avoids any notions of having gained "credit" for obedience to God's Word. We are thankful for victories realized and joyous in gaining ground through warfare, but we have little reason to be elated with ourselves for having begun to attend to a neglected duty.

Distinct Assignments

It was November 1973. Watergate and Vietnam were wrenching the soul of the United States of America. It was on a Wednesday night during that month that the Holy Spirit engraved upon our hearts the responsibility to pray for our land.

A word of prophecy stirred in my soul as I stood to teach from the Bible. I suddenly saw God's commission and my heart ignited with His passion:

"If my people who are called by My name will humble themselves, and pray and seek My face, and turn from their wicked ways, then I will hear from heaven, and will forgive their sin and heal their land."   2 Chronicles 7:14

Then I spoke with Holy Spirit anointing in the name of the Lord: "The Lord says, I am calling this congregation to pray for your nation, and I am calling you to pray as though no other church were praying. I do not say to you that no others *are* praying, but that you are to pray as *though* no others were. If you will keep My word in this matter, I will fulfill My promise."

The "word" was much longer than that, including much exhortation and a call to repentance, especially because passivity in intercession is characteristic of so many of us all. And while our response was not at all great at first, we accepted this call. We were yet to learn the meaning and price of true intercession, and to understand exactly all that our response would require.

The importance of believers praying *continually* for their land did not dawn upon me fully until this time. It started that night after the Holy Spirit had given us that word. One of the elders passed me a slip of paper with a Scripture reference on it, and though the passage was familiar, it was not until that moment that I was struck with its full force:

> Therefore I exhort *first of all* that supplications, prayers, intercessions, and giving of thanks be made for all men, for kings and all who are in authority, that we may lead a quiet and peaceable life in all godliness and reverence.
>   1 Timothy 2:1–2 (author's emphasis)

First of all! I had never noticed it before! This kind of

praying is given as a priority for the entire Church! The implications are frighteningly profound, too. The text says it explicitly: *A society will enjoy "a quiet and peaceable life" only in a nation where the Church is carrying its intercessory responsibility for the land and its leaders!*

With that, we began a pilgrimage in learning the meaning of intercession—a pilgrimage that continues to this day. Joy Dawson has defined *intercession* as "Holy Spirit-directed and Holy Spirit-empowered prayer." That is what we began learning—to seek and to allow the Holy Spirit's revealing to us *what* to pray for and *how* to go about it. Just as we had learned more about prayer as a result of that one request concerning the earthquake, so we are now learning new dimensions of prayer every week concerning our nation's life and neediness.

It was at this juncture that the Holy Spirit moved us to do something in addition to prayer as intercessors for the nation. He called us to enlist others in national intercession. Without any superciliousness, we began to reach out in Jesus' name to do what we could to unite the Church across the nation in emergency prayer for our torn country. Two of our members, Jim and Carol Owens—renowned and beloved composers—wrote a teaching musical embodying the principles of intercessory prayer for *our* nation and for *nations*. The result was "If My People . . . ," a vehicle so effective in leading people to intercessory prayer that we felt God directing us as a congregation to give it to the Church across our land.

It would require another book to report the agony and ecstasy, the tears and the triumphs of that project. But we sent forth a national touring group—a crew of fifty musicians, singers and technicians—who presented concerts in more than 65 major cities across the United States. They sang from the Sports Arena in Los Angeles to the steps of the Capitol in Washington, D.C.; and as they did, our congregation guaranteed the whole budget for the project—six months long in all. As we all stood together in faith, miracles began to take place. Others rallied to support us as well, and every need was met. Best of all, hundreds of thousands responded with abiding commitments to national intercession. A God-given mission and vision had been fulfilled.

What happened as a result?

It is impossible to say, but this much is clear. When we began to pray, social and political analysts were saying that the U.S. was undergoing its greatest time of national division and turmoil since the Civil War. Three years later, after the Church in this country had moved to prayer, even the most cynical journalists agreed that "a new spirit" had come to our nation. Some had said that the 1976 Bicentennial celebration might have become our national funeral; but, in fact, we enjoyed something of a social stability and a measure of peace.

May God alone be praised.

A Wednesday Night Visit

I have mentioned that each of the three weekly primary public services follows basic patterns appropriate to its emphasis. Perhaps a look at a Wednesday night might be a helpful point of seeing how things we have noted can be applied.

It is seven o'clock Wednesday evening and the room is humming with excitement. The family is together and fellowship is being enjoyed as people are arriving from either their homes or workplaces—having won yet another wrestling match with the L.A. traffic. A few remarks are made to draw the people together, and then we begin to sing praises to God—high praises and triumphant anthems. We are coming to declare Christ's dominion in the heavenlies and the music says it all. The mood is set by Psalm 149 which outlines the privileged authority of saints over the adversaries of the Lord:

> Let the high praises of God be in their mouth, and a two-edged sword in their hand, to execute vengeance upon the heathen, and punishments upon the enemy; to bind their authorities with chains and fetters of iron; to exact the judgment that has already been written: this honor belongs to the saints of God—Hallelujah!
>
> Psalm 149:6–9 (author's paraphrase)

As a rule, praiseful worship continues for about a quarter hour, sometimes a mixture of praise, prayer and possibly a prophetic utterance.

We baptize people in water Wednesday and Sunday nights, so the introduction of these candidates occurs here—and the sense of Christ's triumph is expanded. We worship while these are baptized, and following that we come to our intercession time. With our Bibles opened, the text undergirding the evening's specific point of national, international or communitywide intercession is addressed. We define how and on what biblical grounds we should press this point in prayer.

Then, for another ten or fifteen minutes, the entire congregation kneels to pray. Each person partners with another and then we all pray together as one of the pastoral team members leads us to intercede for the matter outlined. This season concludes as we rise in a praiseful musical declaration—"We Exalt Thee" or "Our God Reigns" or "To God Be the Glory"—as we declare the victory of faith!

Next we move toward an interactive prayer time, bearing each other's burdens. *Ministrytime* is the term we use for that segment in many of our services. It has been a stretching point for newcomers to the church, but the most beautiful thing about our prayer circles is that they establish a springboard for ministry. They give each of us practice at listening to others, then finding the Holy Spirit's help to frame prayers appropriate to the needs discussed. In this setting, too, the Lord takes opportunity to give people Scripture passages and ideas that speak to the needs of the people.

We also distribute cards on which prayer requests may be written, and as we handle these, we often suggest how we might learn to pray for such varied matters. Irrespective of how many cards we actually pray for in the service, we put all of them in the Prayer Chapel afterward where intercessors will continue to attend to them that week.

By this time, an hour has passed almost without notice. Then, for 35 to 45 minutes, the evening's teaching from the Word follows—and now it is drawing near 8:45 P.M. The children in the nursery and the grade school kids are waiting for their parents. We dismiss and the commission is given again—"Love one another, church!"

Less than two hours have gone by. But in that time,

the whole world has been impacted, changed because of what has gone on here. The fellowship of saints has sent forth the firepower of the Savior. The Holy Spirit of intercession is a Spirit of travail; and where we travail in prayer, life comes forth and the Kingdom of God extends its triumph over the works of darkness.

Notes

[1] 2 Chronicles 20:15.

[2] These references are only examples. The body of truth supporting these convictions is far broader.

[3] The authority being applied in our intercessory pursuits, however, is not less bold, but is certainly without arrogance. The problem with certain ideas about "faith," as it seems to be emphasized in some quarters, is that many hearers too often translate these truths into "using faith" as a tool to "get the things I want." Well-meaning proponents who misfire with this emphasis, however, wind up cultivating a very real form of "Christianized" selfishness and self-righteousness.

Among devotees in this genre of sincere but sidetracked believers, the test of faith too often becomes one's ability to demonstrate a "product" (healing, money, a new car) with too little concern for maturity or character. Testimonies tend to center on "what I got," and seldom place much value on "how I grew," "what I learned through trial" or "how I overcame smallness of heart or mind."

[4] An elaboration of these ideas is in the author's book *Prayer Is Invading the Impossible,* and may be ordered at your bookstore or from Living Way Ministries. For information, write Living Way Ministries, 14480 Sherman Way, Van Nuys, CA 91405.

[5] In fact, we hold classes, choir practice and other meetings on Wednesday night—but the prayer meeting is the central event.

[6] Romans 8:18–21.

[7] Today we use an overhead projection screen to focus intercessory prayer targets.

13

Members of His Body

She was sweet, beautifully simple and obviously sincere. And noticing that this twenty-something girl had signed the visitors' guestbook in the foyer of the church, I read her entry following the service as I was positioning myself at the door to speak to worshipers as they left.

Beside her name in the space inviting the indication of one's "Church Home," she had written: "The Body of Christ!" As the "Location" of her church she had entered: "Worldwide."

I chuckled to myself as I glanced at her entry, but felt bad, too. Her entry, sincerely intended as I am sure it was, was also sadly representative of the unsupportable, hollow ideas some dear people have about church relationship. It is not uncommon to find people whose notion of membership in the church is either equally as ethereal as that young lady's or, worse, downright resistant. Sadder is the fact that some see this uncommitment as somehow distinguishing, as though revealing some higher order of spirituality or spiritual insight.

I did not say anything to her about it. We simply exchanged a pleasantry or two about the service (which she admitted to enjoying), and then she was gone. I do not know that I ever saw her again; perhaps she found a church home. But even if she did, I wonder if she would have joined.

The memory of that young woman has stuck. She represents a contingent of believers who are unquestionably devoted to Jesus Christ, but who never identify with His Body, at least in the sense of a local commitment; they never join a church. I hasten to assert that joining a church is not an unspiritual idea at all. "Join" is exactly what every member of our physical body does, to connect it with other members for effective functioning. Since that physical figure—the "Body," "members," "every one of us"—is all through the New Testament, we see joining a local body simply as a commitment to a biblical idea. It is a person's way of saying, "This is where the Lord wants me to function in relationship with other members of Jesus' Body."

Naturally, I am fully aware of the wide spectrum of reasons for not joining a church. They range from the scars some still bear—from wounds inflicted in another church relationship—to deep devastation from church infighting, including petty criticism, doctrinal accusations or a big one: the domestic tragedy of a divorce compounded by ecclesiastical ostracism. This kind of hurt often leaves an unholy "hangover" regarding church membership. And besides the wounded, others simply reject the idea of membership out of hand, mocking joining a church as a cheapening exercise, indicating that those who acknowledge formal church membership have taken a spiritual matter and reduced it to a piece of paper.

I have pastored too long not to understand these problems.

But I have also shepherded too long to believe that any sheep is safe without accepting the Holy Spirit's direction to settle down with one local flock and receive care and feeding in a faithful pastorate.

Not long after meeting that young woman in the foyer, I was musing over her guestbook entry, and thinking how often the Church is referred to in military metaphors in the Bible. I imagined the following scenario:

Location: The streets of Oxford, England.

Scene: A U.S. Military Police jeep stops. One of the patrol team jumps to the pavement and approaches an American soldier weaving unevenly down the sidewalk.

M.P.: (sharply) *Soldier, halt! Where are you going?*

G.I.: (muttering) *Nowhere . . . next bar.*

M.P.: *Looks to me like you'd better be headed back to your base. Where are you stationed?*

G.I.: *Nowhere particular. Wherever.*

M.P.: (to partner in jeep) *This guy's spaced, Corporal.* (to G.I.) *Hold it, soldier. Again: Where's your base? Who's your commanding officer?*

G.I.: *Hey, man. I told you.* (stops, draws to full stature) *I'm in the U.S. military. We're worldwide, haven't you heard? I'm stationed wherever I happen to go—I'm in THE Army, man. Global.*

M.P.: *You're drunk, fella. Where are your papers? Who's your commanding officer?*

G.I.: *The President, man. The Commander-in-Chief. You know, in D.C.—at headquarters.*

Enough. The whole proposition is bizarre. And if the situation actually occurred, there is no doubt where the soldier would be within fifteen minutes: the brig.

The Bible on "Membership"

The irony of the analogy is its similarity to the thinking of many who, as innocent as they may be, are nonetheless ignorant of the biblical concepts of *membership, submission* to leadership and *union* with a local assembly in abiding fellowship.

True, the Church of Jesus Christ is worldwide. And Jesus is the Lord—"Commander-in-Chief," if you please. But just as surely as a soldier in military service needs a base to ensure function and accountability, so an individual believer in Jesus needs identification with a local assembly. This is not to deny our desire for unity with the global Body of Christ. Church membership does not mean we remove ourselves from commitment to Jesus' whole Body, while retreating to a sectarian bigotry or denominational pridefulness; and neither does church membership substitute a pastor or a group for the Lordship of Christ in our lives. No, the practical realities of membership we are dealing with are those that can be clearly seen in the Word of God.

To become a member of a church is not a bureaucratic experience, it is a spiritual one, and our congregation has tried to do our utmost to keep it that way. Since we believe that *joining* is a biblical term, we try to be sensitive as to how we receive members the Holy Spirit is adding (that is, "joining") to our assembly.

Just as a limb connects at a joint, so we believe that the scriptural figure indicates that each member added to a local assembly is in fact "joined" with that assembly. We believe that human relationships are important for the growth of Christ's purpose in our lives; that being knit to this local part of His worldwide Body is as specific and significant a placement as a physical transplant (or a military base assignment!).

Ephesians 4:15–16 is graphic in its use of anatomical terminology:

> Speaking the truth in love, [we] may grow up in all things into Him who is the head—Christ—from whom the whole body, joined and knit together by what every joint supplies, . . . causes growth of the body for the edifying of itself in love.

These inspired words of Scripture teach a dependence upon one another that we all need to acknowledge—a mutual dependence that results in healthy growth. Such growth is not practical outside of a person's commitment to a body of believers.

Our need for fellowship is further underscored in Paul's 1 Corinthians 12:15–16 analogy: No one can properly say, "Because I am one distinct member (an eye, for example), I have no need of you." The issue cannot be dodged. I cannot be biblical about membership and still say, "I don't need this!" Even though the context says, "By one Spirit we are all baptized into one body," that statement, while acknowledging the fundamental unity of the whole, does not negate our dependence on the parts. Instead, it accents the need for integrated relationships in the Body—right where we live.

The same epistle teaches how submission to local leadership is important. Paul shows that even within the larger believing community of all Christians in Corinth, individual believers were still aligned with specific smaller groups. Writing to believers in that city, he urges every person to "submit" himself to a spiritual leader who could be trusted. He uses Stephanas as an example:

> I urge you, brethren—you know the household of Stephanas, that it is the firstfruits of Achaia, and that they have devoted themselves to the ministry of the saints—that you also submit to such, and to everyone who works and labors with us.
>
> 1 Corinthians 16:15–16

Background on a Problem

The primary problem for people who resist commitment to a local assembly may be the fact that church membership is clearly not a requirement for one's personal salvation. Some people became members of a church before they were born again, and were never told the difference between a relationship with Jesus and a relationship with a church. These people are understandably wary of membership after they have found a meaningful relationship with Christ. They sometimes fear that a formal church membership now, since they have been truly born again, might deprive them of something of the joy and reality they have come to know in Him. So, because membership is often stressed in circles where vital spiritual experience is not, some of today's church leaders hesitate even to suggest the idea of membership for fear of seeming unspiritual.

I had to work through that line of thought myself.

"After all," the argument goes, "since the true reality of membership is actually in the spiritual realm, why not leave it there? Forget the trivia of keeping books and rolls. Paperwork may just bewilder people. It might also discourage those who are finally tasting freshness and joy after years of barrenness elsewhere." Thus, fear postures itself, proposing that formal membership might taint a beautiful experience and cripple a sincere person with human methodologies or arthritic organizational structures.

At first this might sound plausible, but it lacks both biblical and logical grounds. It is as unreasonable as refusing to plan a reception after a wedding because you once saw a reception turn into a drunken brawl.

Actually, the reception of members into a local church family is not unlike a wedding reception. Here we are acknowledging believers' union with Christ, distinctly rejoicing that He has placed them in our local part of His great family. We welcome them to growth, fellowship and fruitful partnership. What has already been accomplished when they vowed their lives to Christ we joyously acknowledge, and it is in that joy that we receive them openly and lovingly.

The Bible establishes the wisdom of this principle, and logic supports it.

If church membership is too spiritual a matter to be sullied by institutionalism, what about love and the civil rite of marriage? Is the texture of true love sacrificed when vows are exchanged at the altar? Or when the documents are signed? Or when the union is recorded in the county courthouse?

The idea that a couple does not have to commit to marriage is popular today, of course, but not among those of us who are believers in Christ and heed God's Word. Since a formal public commitment may properly *and spiritually* crown a courtship and its season of romance, why shouldn't a public commitment to a specific church family enrich rather than diminish a person's experience with Jesus Christ?

Spiritual experience involves two things: an internal, private realization, and an external, public expression. When the Spirit of God draws us to faith and repentance, for example, we must express it openly through confession and baptism. In other words, the *inner* witness of the Holy Spirit that we are indeed children of God[1] does not end the matter.[2] The Word calls for us to enlarge our circle of witness. We are commanded: "Confess with your mouth" as well as "Believe in your heart." Following this, *spiritual* faith becomes *physical*—practical and, if you will, "formal." Further, water baptism is commanded by Jesus as yet another formal *physical* acknowledgment of an inner *spiritual* work of faith.[3] Since this physical or visible pattern is so obvious as a part of the new birth of the believer, it should not seem any less spiritual that the same pattern leads to the believer's relationship with a local congregation. When I have been *born* into the family of God, I know so and say so. Similarly, when I find my place to *live* in that family, I should know so and say so.

The Goal Is Growth

Here at The Church On The Way we are convinced that commitment to church membership contributes to the growth of a believer. While we by no means consider it essential to salvation, we have found that the act of commitment usually blossoms into new personal developments of ministry and growth. So when we receive members, we truly believe we are participating in a spiritual activity, not merely an institutional one.

Despite our deep convictions about the biblical basis and practical wisdom of church membership, we virtually never do anything to demand or promote it. Nonetheless, multiplied thousands have submitted to membership since Anna and I joined the church ourselves at the time we became its pastors.

My own understanding of the deep significance of this practice grew with time, but not because I felt I had to answer to a human or denominational tradition. In fact, I challenged the idea, searching the Word of God. The way we began to receive members was the result of my study, which brought a growing perception of certain spiritual principles. Today we continue our quest to implement those principles with sensitivity, consistency and spiritual dynamic—a procedure born out of our early experiences at the church.

The first full flush of growth at the church came within the first three years, and I wrestled with the issue of membership. Refusing to acquiesce to the idea that membership is unspiritual, I asked the Lord to help me perceive it from His viewpoint. A biblical picture became my answer, helping me to clarify the issue in my own heart.

In Israel and the Middle East, where the Bible was mostly written, the figure of sheep and shepherds was used to describe certain spiritual principles. Following this example, it is a fact that shepherds "know their sheep," and that they both mark and count them. We should be consistent to "mark" and keep an accounting of our sheep, too. Jesus Christ is the Lord—the Owner of every member of the flock, having bought each sheep with His own blood. But He has also assigned certain of His sheep to my care; and in order for me to know those who are under my charge, the mark of membership becomes a point of accountability—for me, the "shepherd," and for each member "sheep," too.

Thus, membership does not indicate human ownership but an acknowledged corporate relationship. "I belong" could be twisted into a cliquish taunt, but our "I belong" has come to mean, "I am committed and I am responsible to." With that view of church membership, we began to offer its possibility in the following way:

On Submitting to Membership

Each month, we simply place a notice in the church bulletin announcing the date and location of a four-hour seminar, through which we will receive people into membership. At that gathering, we also present the requirements of membership:

1. You have received Jesus Christ as your Savior (John 3:3–5; Romans 10:9–10).

2. You agree with the church's statement of faith (2 Timothy 3:10–4:4).

3. You will support the congregation's ministry with tithes, offerings and intercessory prayer (Malachi 3:8–12; Ephesians 6:10–20).

4. You want to serve the Lord Jesus and will wait on

Him to disclose to you your place of ministry in the ongoing life of our fellowship (Ephesians 4:15–16; 1 Corinthians 12:12–31).

As a rule, we make no public announcements apart from this written notice. We depend on the Holy Spirit to move people to acknowledge that He is drawing them to submit to and unite with this assembly. This way we can deal confidently and authoritatively with those who respond, for our base of authority is not our own solicitation or influence but God's work in people's hearts.

In making even a passing mention of "our authority," I am inclined to wince, for the domination exercised in some church traditions has often violated the Spirit of Christ and the intent of God's Word regarding pastoral authority. Still, in the epistle to the Hebrews, the practice of acknowledging one's submission to pastoral leadership is reinforced. At the same time, however, the Scriptures emphasize the awesome responsibility and accountability we leaders will have before God:

> Obey them that lead you, and submit yourselves, for they are responsible to watch for your souls as ones who must give an account before God for their leadership responsibility.
>
> Hebrews 13:17 (author's paraphrase)

This text notes that submittedness is required not only of the members, but also of their leaders. Pastors, elders and other officers are responsible to acknowledge their membership in a body as well, and submit to its authority.

It is a worthy point of study to see how Paul, Titus and

Barnabas submitted their flourishing ministry among the Gentiles to the evaluative, corrective judgment of the leaders in Jerusalem (see Galatians 2:1–2, 9). Similarly, Paul and Barnabas gave an accounting to Antioch about the mission to which that church had commissioned them (Acts 14:26–28). They were not itinerants; they were accountable to their home base. They were not maverick evangelists operating like Lone Rangers; they were "sent"—commissioned at the command of the Holy Spirit and under the authority of a home church.

When we teach about submission, we reject emphatically puppet-producing hierarchical authoritarianism. We believe deeply that each person's ministry is released most fully when that person is functioning under representative headship. This term means that though the Lord Jesus Christ places people as leaders in His Church, they do not substitute for Him; rather, they represent Him. In that role they are *assistants* to the Head— teaching voices under the Holy Spirit and trustworthy examples accountable to God.

> And He Himself [Christ, the ascended Lord] gave some to be apostles, some prophets, some evangelists, and some pastors and teachers.
>
> Ephesians 4:11

> The elders who are among you I exhort: feed the flock of God which is among you, serving as their overseers, not by constraint but willingly; not for dishonest gain but eagerly. Do not lord over those entrusted to you, but be examples to the flock; and when our Chief Shepherd Jesus appears, you will receive the crown of glory that will not fade away.
>
> 1 Peter 5:1–4 (author's paraphrase)

All headship, then, which Christ has placed in His Church as a gift to His Church is answerable to Him. He has given:

1. *Ministries,* qualified by gift and then placed by His own hand *to assist His Body toward ministry* (Ephesians 4:11–12);

2. *Elders,* who serve and oversee the flock without selfish or material motivation, *providing mature influence* by reason of their spiritual commitment and growth (1 Peter 5:1–2);

3. *Shepherds* responsible to the Chief Shepherd who exemplify His quality of life to the sheep and *who lay down their lives* in loving, servant-like self-giving (1 Peter 5:3–4).

Reception into Membership

When people come to join the church, we emphasize that in doing so they are saying, "The Holy Spirit led me to do this." We want them to be sure *He* has placed them here to work in coordination with the whole body.

They are submitting, therefore, first to God, second to pastoral leadership and third to the local assembly. When they acknowledge their submission, we respond by submitting ourselves to them as well, for the Bible teaches that submission is the mutual responsibility of all believers: "[Submit yourselves] to one another in the fear of God" (Ephesians 5:21).

When receiving members, we make the commitment summarized in this statement:

In responding to your trust, and in submitting to you as your servant and pastor, on behalf of the pastoral staff and the elder body, we receive you into the membership of the congregation. In doing this we affirm these commitments:

Instruction: First, we commit ourselves as pastors to teach and feed you the pure Word of God (John 21:16). We who pastor you believe in the absolute need of your knowing and growing in the Word of God. We will give ourselves to nourish you, with the goal that you become the maximum possible person according to Father God's plan for your life.

Correction: Second, in that same regard, we are committed to counseling or correcting you, should you ever drift from "the truth as it is in Jesus." The Bible directs pastoral leadership to "reprove, rebuke, exhort with all long suffering and doctrine" (2 Timothy 4:2, KJV). We are committed to doing everything lovingly possible to keep you in obedience to the Lord Jesus Christ.

Intercession: Third, we commit ourselves to pray for you. The Bible says we are to "shepherd the flock" and to "watch out for your souls" (1 Peter 5:2; Hebrews 13:17). We will uphold you in regular intercessory prayer as we, the pastors and elders, continually bring the congregation to God's throne.

Protection: Fourth, we commit ourselves to standing by you in any time of need, burden or personal crisis. In the early Church, no one said that the things they had were selfishly, solely their own (Acts 4:32). By that, we understand that according to New Testament life, any material need you may have is ours to bear with you also. You will never be alone if you will let us know when hard times arise.

Devotion: Finally, we commit ourselves to loving

you. Jesus said that this trait should mark His disciples (John 13:35), and we intend to live out that divine order of love. Its essence is not so much in affection as in commitment. Affection depends upon personal acquaintance; and, given time, we may enjoy such growth in the purity and beauty of getting to know you better. But regardless of how close *socially* we may or may not become, we are always *personally* committed to you. Should you ever feel you have been hurt, neglected or misunderstood, you will know it is unintentional, because we will never do anything to violate you in any way. Our total commitment is to love, serve and help you become the person God created you to be.

Reception: I extend the right hand of fellowship to you, and in Jesus' name receive you into this assembly. Please know that you are loved and received.

Then we embrace each one. We strongly believe that both *the right hand of fellowship*[4] and *the holy embrace*[5] are dynamic spiritual expressions. If ministered in the love and power of the Holy Spirit, they become means of confirming a vital moment when a spiritual union is established between the one being received and the assembly to which they are being joined.

Responsible Membership

Most people do not join a church until they have attended for several months. This provides opportunity to understand the requirements and responsibilities of membership. We expect primarily that people will give themselves to growing into Christ's purpose for them. We do not dictate how an individual should pursue this purpose. If Jesus has called them to Himself and to this local fellowship, however, it follows that they will help in ministries that advance their personal calling and serve the congregation's needs.

Here is how we relate our requirements and responsibilities for membership:

First Requirement: To be born again, having received Jesus Christ, the Son of God, as your own Savior and Lord.

Corresponding responsibilities: To commit yourself continually to growth in Christ, and to pursue willingly biblical standards in your life.

Second Requirement: To be in agreement with the congregation's statement of faith—the Declaration of Faith of the Foursquare Church.[6]

Corresponding responsibilities: To seek to live in the fullness of the Holy Spirit, the most excellent way to live in the truth you confess, and to manifest the fruit and gifts of His life within.

Third Requirement: To support the congregation's ministry continually with your prayer, intercession, tithes and offerings.

Corresponding responsibilities: To accept a personal place in prayer and intercession, and to grow into the freedom of giving with the minimum of the biblical tithe (ten percent) as your starting point (Malachi 3:10).

Fourth Requirement: To wait on your ministry, seeking to discern the will of God for your life and service as part of this body.

Corresponding responsibilities: To be available every day as a Holy Spirit-directed minister of

Christ's Kingdom love and life; to be involved in the fellowship of one of our congregation's LIFE-NET (small) groups; and to help actively in practical ways by serving the needs of the congregation.

If any membership candidate has not yet been baptized in water, he is expected to be before becoming a member. We do not require a person to have been baptized in our church, but we do believe, teach and urge that every believer be baptized in water *after* he or she has received Jesus Christ as Savior.[7]

We do not hawkishly monitor each individual's follow-through to these membership duties. Our overseeing is established for everyone's care, not to ensure their busyness. But our requirements and responsibilities do provide a clearly marked pathway of expectations for disciples, and the majority choose to pursue it faithfully. They recognize it is founded on the Word and respond because it is ministered in a living, growing way.

Two sets of chorus lyrics seem to underscore the spirit of our reception when we receive new members:

> We are bound to each other in love,
> By the words of the Father above.
> Through the blood of His Son,
> We are merged into one;
> We are bound to each other in love.[8]

> It's a new and living way, walk ye in it.
> It's a new and living way God has planned.
> In this new and living way,
> I am walking day by day;
> Protected and led by His right hand.[9]

It is not difficult to maintain joy in a "joined" church relationship when that kind of love and that kind of life are the theme.

Notes

1 Romans 8:16.

2 Romans 10:9–10.

3 Matthew 28:19.

4 Galatians 2:9.

5 2 Corinthians 13:12, *et. al.*

6 Should any reader be interested, a copy will be mailed if you write to The Church On The Way, 14300 Sherman Way, Van Nuys, CA 91405. (Please enclose $2 for handling costs.)

7 See Jack Hayford, *Newborn* (Wheaton, Ill.: Tyndale House Publishers, 1984).

8 Eli Chavira, used with permission.

9 Author unknown.

14

Follow the Rainbow

By the time I arrived, a congregation of well over a thousand was already there—summer clothes in bright profusion, kids running or playing in wild confusion and fellowship's joy flowing like a spiritual effusion. This Sunday afternoon picnic was scheduled to climax with our regular 5:30 evening service there on the sprawling lawns of Emmaus Park.

It was the Fourth of July weekend, but the festive spirit had to do with more than either the holiday weekend or the picnic setting. The joyous peace amid the raucous sounds of kids at play was the fruit of obedience. As surely as we feel its reward when we have personally obeyed God in a private matter, so any group of the Lord's people feels His approval when they have given themselves to His will in a conscious, concerted way. *Yes, I thought to myself, this gathering is happy and fun, both! But I know the sheer joy all over this place is due to answering Your call, Lord.*

It was an exciting setting, one that had actually begun,

in a way, at a commuter station in Japan several months before.

During rush hour, Tokyo's Shinjuku railroad terminal is a cross between Houston's NASA Space Center during a countdown and the Indianapolis 500. As trains shake the ground, rumbling up to the station's multiple platforms, each car stops just in time to belch forth a cluster of humanity. Doors slither open mechanically and the tide of human bodies pouring out seems to form a phalanx as people move in troop-like rhythm, striding toward ramps and doorways leading to places of work on nearby streets or to another train poised and waiting to leap away. It is done every single workday at Shinjuku, where Japanese ingenuity, combined with that people's penchant for regimentation and synchronization, choreographs the pickup and delivery of more than two million passengers per business day—at that one site! As I stood back, pressing against the side wall of one of the huge tunnels through which the droves flowed, I was within speaking distance of the more than 25,000 people who passed me in fewer than fifteen minutes.

Aside from being impressed by the sheer efficiency of management, precision in timing, coordination and crowd control, I was most moved by the raw presence of this great mobile mass of humanity.

I was in Japan at the request of ministries there, speaking daily to pastors who had come from many towns and cities to one of the three conferences being held in Nagoya, Kyoto and here in Tokyo. But though I was in Japan on business, I had come to Shinjuku as a tourist— just to watch. And now my heart was throbbing. I felt the heart of God for multitudes. I was moved personally just studying the faces of hundreds who hurried by, each one a unique representation of the blended intensity, delicacy and creativity that characterizes these remarkable people.

But now, this summer day in Emmaus Park, I was standing in the middle of crowds of kids and picnicking parents, and the happy glow surrounding the crowd had a reason. We were beginning to answer the call to "multitudes" and my Shinjuku visit had been a contributor to this fact.

I say Shinjuku, but of course it had been the Lord dealing with me there. I had not had a vision. I did not hear any words. In fact, I did not even talk with anyone. But I had the experience of feeling something like what I suppose Matthew meant that Jesus felt: "When He saw the multitudes, He was moved with compassion for them, because they were weary and scattered, like sheep having no shepherd."[1]

As a consequence of His feeling that compassion, the Gospel writer reports Jesus' doing two things. First, He called His disciples to pray: "Pray the Lord of the harvest to send out laborers into His harvest." Second, He trained His disciples to commission them to broader ministry.

Our congregation had already experienced a handful of years in being helped to see ourselves as "ministers"—agents of Christ. But now the Holy Spirit was prodding us forward, this being the first of a new series of dealings focusing on ministry outreach. It is something the Holy Spirit has done several times and in different ways, renewing His grace in our midst and keeping us from ingrown attitudes. On this occasion we were facing up to the impossibility of ministering to multitudes if we ever became bound to a "building orientation": only "bringing the crowd in" without "going into all the world."

Anytime God begins blessing a group of people, it is easy for the passage of time to bring a preoccupation with the phenomenon itself. Even a growing church can suppose it is beyond the proclivity we humans have for introversion. While no "cliquishness" had overtaken us yet, I had recognized a subtle tendency toward self-centeredness. A crowd whose focus centers on God's throne, just as Isaiah's did when he was overwhelmed by a vision of His glory, is no less needful than that prophet was to hear God say, *Who will go?*

Here on the lawns were hosts who had begun to give Isaiah's answer: "Here am I, send me!"

It was feeling very good in this place. Intermittently the Lord Jesus lifts our heads and reanoints our eyes to see the world's need. This is important because it is possible to become so entranced with the ecstasy of glory that we forget the agony of people who only dream of it in the dark night of their need.

So this gathering was a celebration of joy over a recent outreach we had made. We considered this event to be a statement: We were "on the way" in a new sense, committed to an expanding readiness to be what He was calling us to be.

The Rainbow

There was a special exhilarating quality to the hugs and happy greetings Anna and I received as we walked across the grounds, stopping to meet one nucleus of people after another. Smiles seemed brighter, embraces more loving. Indeed, though the words were not spoken aloud, everyone sensed a holy witness confirming the Father's blessing on our commitment to answer His present call to us as a body.

I had made my way to the pavilion area where about three hundred children were entranced by a puppet show. Wayne was teaching—dynamically, humorously, effectively as usual—captivating everyone present with the tender touch of grace on his ministry. I was standing at the back door to avoid distracting anyone, when one of our teenagers ran up to me, laughing excitedly. "Pastor Jack, did you see the rainbow?"

My eyes followed her pointing finger to the multicolored arch directly overhead.

"Isn't that somethin', Pastor Jack?" she emoted. "It's just as though the Lord is saying He's pleased, isn't it!"

I hesitated, not wanting to lend too much credence to a proposition that could be based upon mere happenstance. But then I smiled.

"Yes," I replied, looking up again intently. "It sure is."

I hugged the kid, and she ran off again to join the crowd, leaving me there alone.

As I was starting to turn back to the puppet show, I was caught mid-step. The Lord spoke: *Tell the people that it is true. The rainbow* is *a sign from Me. It is a response to their obedience, and a sign of My blessing upon them.* With this strong directive, I also sensed I was to relay another word He had whispered to my heart three months before, the night before Easter.

I had been at prayer in the sanctuary, inviting God's blessing on the events of the next day's grand celebrations. While there that evening, I was especially sensitized to His calling us to reach out—to learn to *go* to the multitudes. But as we did, I was moved with one passion: "Whatever You plan for us, Lord, my one request is that

Your glory always attend and cover us; for the only reason we have anything at all is because of that gift You have given us."

His gentle, heart-firming words responded to my prayer with the immediate grace of this promise. He answered: *My glory shall go before you. My glory shall rest upon you like a mantle. And My glory shall be your rereward.*[2]

I wept.

Now, several weeks later, I still had mentioned this to only a very few. But as I glanced upward at the rainbow again, I knew I had to tell the people two things: first, of that word on Easter eve and, second, that the rainbow was God's seal of approval on our willingness to remain obedient to reach out to others.

I trembled slightly. I felt somewhat awkward—exposed to possible misunderstanding. I had just been put under assignment to relate something that I felt could likely test the credulity of many intelligent yet spiritually minded people. For although we do believe in the supernatural, I have been slow to assign too much significance to things that some might snatch gullibly or superstitiously as signs.

I looked at my watch: It was 4:30. In just one hour the crowd would gather on the grassy field for a time of worship and Communion together. My feelings were in conflict, much as Sheldon Vanauken describes his own following an experience when his wife was near death.

Vanauken tells how a rainbow had suddenly appeared one day, and upon seeing it he had the deepest feeling it had been intended as a personal assuring sign of comfort to him. In his book *A Severe Mercy,* he not only relates feeling that assurance, but describes his intellectualized bouts over having allowed the feeling. Trying to resolve his dilemma as to whether he was merely yielding to sentiment or to God, he wrote his friend C. S. Lewis, expressing his mixture of faith and doubt about the rainbow.

Lewis' answer magnificently characterizes the life and thought of that giant mind; having the intellectual respect of all his colleagues at both Oxford and Cambridge universities in their time, he still related to God's grace and love in Christ with the faith of a child. His brilliant faith and humility of intellect shine in his reply to Vanauken:

> I can't now remember what I said in my lost letter about the "Signs." My general view is that, once we have accepted an omniscient and providential God, the distinction we used to draw between the significant and the fortuitous must either break down or be restated in some very much subtler form. If an event coming about in the ordinary course of nature becomes to me the occasion of hope and faith and love or increased efforts after virtue, do we suppose that this result was unforeseen by, or is indifferent to, God? Obviously not. What we should have called its fortuitous effects must have been present to Him for all eternity.[3]

Now I was being called to a similar commitment to faith, that this "fortuitous" appearance of the rainbow was indeed a token of God's providence and pleasure. I began to feel the assurance that if I told the people what He was saying to me, the Lord would cause them to see it was more than mere sentiment or superstition.

The 5:30 worship began with singing and praise, and

shortly it was time for me to lead us all to observe the Lord's Table as we had planned. The midsummer sun was lowering and extending lengthening shadows across the field. I began by asking everyone to quiet their children.

The congregation stilled itself, and I set myself to deliver the message God had given me. I took time first to express my natural reluctance to share what I was about to bring. But at the same time I affirmed my conviction that God wanted us to receive a confirming sign with the simplicity of children.

I then recounted my experience at Eastertime, of God's promise of abiding glory—to go before and behind us as we obeyed Him. From there I moved on, preparing to describe the prompting He had given me about the rainbow.

Then, with between one and two thousand people looking on, one of the most incredible events of my life took place.

It was now just past six o'clock and I was retelling my conversation with the teenager who had run up excitedly to talk with me about the rainbow at 4:30. Everyone at the picnic had seen the rainbow, which, of course, had long since disappeared. But now, as I was reenacting the conversation, I came to the words "I looked up to see the rainbow," and was about to say, "And the Lord spoke to me. . . ." Then, at that very moment before the gathered crowd, as I lifted my head looking upward to dramatize that earlier conversation, *another rainbow was shimmering directly overhead!*

I was stunned.

My speech faltered momentarily, prompting every eye to look upward, and as we all did, a holy murmur swept across the congregation. I fumbled for words. It was beyond imagination—we all knew it. In my speechless sense of awe, I did do one thing right: I invited everyone to kneel and worship the Lord.

Nothing foolish took place, but it was not very neatly handled. I was too overwhelmed. We all were. I tried to explain it all somehow and apply it in some way, but was dissatisfied with my verbal attempts. Still, as we proceeded to worship and receive Communion, there was no one present who did not understand what was happening. God was underscoring His promise to overspread us with His glory as long as we were willing to obey, even as our partaking of His Table enunciates that we move outward with our witness and "proclaim the Lord's death till He comes" again.[4]

Risking Belief

One is always at risk to believe in the invisible. Even when the visible evidence confirms your belief in the invisible, it is judged by many as not being intellectual enough, somehow. We are always vulnerable to its being said we are "unscientific" or "fanatical" when we admit that we believe and travel in what others may not judge to be approvable terrain.

A scientist is charged with being inconsistent with his profession when he expresses belief in a personal Creator. A doctor may be thought mystically errant if he refuses spiritual cynicism. That monster of academic arrogance sucks the heart from good people. Esteemed scientific and medical practitioners face a seemingly relentless assault of unbelief, and it is horribly unjust.

The toll on their emotions taken by disease, affliction, pain and death, amid their tireless efforts at stemming these plagues, merits them the privilege of being allowed a reprieve simply to "know God" and love Him.

Even pastors become vulnerable to the accusation of unorthodoxy when they appear to venture too far into the arena of belief in the invisible. Peers will allow a measure of faith in the unseen; but even in the circles of those whose stock-in-trade is supposed to be the supernatural, claiming too much causes uneasiness.

This doubt is explainable. Soothsayers, charlatans and kooks are present in large enough numbers, making wild enough claims, to make it seem safer for someone who has had a *bona fide* spiritual experience reluctant to relate it.

All this notwithstanding, the evidence still mounts, and a person comes to the place that he, as I, must risk being bold enough to tell it outright. In my telling, I hope one factor has distinguished my reports from mere sensationalistic gullibility. Throughout this book, I have sought to anchor every experience in the Word of God— the timeless, eternal Scriptures. The pages of the Bible are laden with episode upon episode of signs, wonders, visions, dreams, prophecies, healings, God speaking with men and women, angels at work, miracles, glory clouds and . . . rainbows. So I hope my reports are seen as unsolicited experiences that do indeed have biblical precedents.

In any case, the week following "our" rainbows, in a more reflective, coherent way than I was able to do that Sunday night, I wrote about the experience in my weekly communiqué to the congregation. I entitled my entry "I Believe in Rainbows."

There are four instances in the Bible in which a rainbow is mentioned: three times are direct references to the glory of God's presence and throne (Ezekiel 1:28; Revelation 4:3, 10:1); and, of course, the fourth—the best-known—is that manifestation to Noah after the deluge (Genesis 9:13–14, 16). The very presence of these references indicates that in each case the writers understood the rainbow to hold genuine spiritual significance.

"But, wait just a minute, mister." (Does your mind protest like mine sometimes?) "Don't you know that a rainbow is just a natural phenomenon, nothing more than the spectrum of color cast by the reflection of light rays passing through water vapor or crystals? C'mon now. You don't mean you believe it has significance! Only the gullible would suggest any divine significance to a rainbow!"

But I do believe.

Not that every one has a pot of gold at its end.

Not that it is some kind of good luck sign.

Nor even that every time one appears there is some historic event to be recorded.

But I do *believe.*

I believe in rainbows. Not only as beautiful, scientifically explainable realities, but *I believe that in every rainbow is a message of God's promise.* His Word tells us He gave the rainbow for that reason— to seal His providential promise to preserve mankind from a repeat of the ancient flood, which exploded such judgment upon global evil.

And there is also an abiding promise in the rainbow. By it, God's promise is conveyed from one generation of the faithful to the next, beginning with Noah until today, and saying to each generation: "The Lord who has preserved you this far will continue to do so."

As you know, Noah lived after the flood for another three hundred years. Can you imagine the remarks of successive generations when heavy rains came: "It's happening again. Head for the hills!" But Noah knew better. He believed in and spoke of the sign.

Then a century or so later, skeptics might have said to him: "Come off it, Noah. Don't tell us that color in the clouds means anything special. I suppose you expect us to believe God has spoken to you—you personally—through that sign in the sky?"

I can imagine it, can you? See them turning to one another as they walk away from Mr. Noah: "Can you figure that guy? Some people! The *audacity* to think that God touches the skies with messages for them! Why, we have been seeing those things for—well, ever since I can remember—but we don't try to ascribe meaning to it like that kook!"

What does the Bible say?

The fact is, it says a lot. Let's look at the other profound passages of rainbow revelation.

Both Ezekiel and John saw rainbows that related to a special presence of God. Read their words. Around six hundred years before Christ, Ezekiel wrote:

"Then I looked, and behold, a whirlwind was coming out of the north, a great cloud with raging fire engulfing itself; and brightness was all around it and radiating out of its midst. . . . From within it came the likeness of four living creatures . . . like the appearance of torches. . . . And above . . . was the likeness of a throne . . . with the appearance of a man high above it [and around him] the appearance of fire with brightness all around. . . . Like the appearance of a rainbow in a cloud on a rainy day."[5]

Compare that with John's words, written about seven hundred years later:

"Immediately I was in the Spirit; and behold, a throne set in heaven, and One sat on the throne. And He who sat there was like a jasper and a sardius stone in appearance; and there was a rainbow around the throne, in appearance like an emerald.... And around the throne, were four living creatures.... And they do not rest day or night, saying, 'Holy, holy, holy, Lord God Almighty, who was and is and is to come!' "[6]

They were not hesitant to acknowledge these manifestations of God's glory, although I suppose people could have told them, "You're seeing things." And the people would have been right: They *were* seeing things, and they believed in both the *reality* and the *significance* of what they were!

And so why should the rainbow over Emmaus Park last Sunday night mean something to us? Why should we believe it was a sign of anything special, indicating God's confirmation of blessing upon us at this stage of our congregation's life?

Should we believe just because there was a rainbow even though there had been no rain?

Should we believe just because it appeared directly over the park—hardly appearing to be wider than the approximate dimensions of the site upon which we gathered?

Should we believe just because it appeared again—phenomenally reappearing one and a half hours later, at the precise moment I was relating

God's word to me that the earlier rainbow was a sign of God's glory promised to us as a people?

Should I believe God might signal His pleasure with our will to obey the Holy Spirit in reaching beyond our walls to the world He loves?

I think so.

And I do.

I do believe that God gave that rainbow to manifest His glory to the congregation, as a distinct and unique sign of His readiness to work with power. I do believe He is confirming His readiness to bless, in response to our readiness to serve Him obediently.

And I also believe that any time God gives a sign, it will always take the same childlike faith to receive it that motivates the loving obedience that causes God to display it.

And I believe something else. I believe that the morning after the Red Sea parted, you could probably have found a few toughminded saints in the Israeli camp, knowingly scratching their chins, and with scientifically approved nods, murmuring to one another, "It must have been the wind. How fortunate."

A Scientist Writes

That was my "biblical case" for believing that the rainbow episode was credible for a Christian to accept without being thought crazy by his peers. But sometime later one of the scientists of our congregation wrote me concerning rainbow occurrences. He noted:

Pastor, the whole phenomenal idea of a rainbow is based around the light of the sun being projected toward a man in a straight line—the axis of projection. If we consider the possibility that the sun may serve as a type or symbol of God, projecting in a straight line—His Truth—to mankind as a promise, then here are some randomly ordered analogies that might illustrate the spiritual significance of a rainbow:

1. The intensity of a rainbow is directly related to the number of raindrops present—the more, the brighter; it is only when a large number of raindrops are seen together that a rainbow can be detected. It is a collective phenomenon, obviously a message on the need for the spirit of unity in the whole Body of Christ.

2. All colors are present in the "white" light of the sun, but white light is refracted—bent—as each believer receives the full glory of God. There is a lesson of God's grace in the fact that each raindrop "bends" the light. All of us, in a sense, due to our sinful nature, bend God's light that impinges upon us. Yet, God is still able to turn that refraction into a work of beauty (Romans 8:28).

3. He is doing this through the Body of Christ, the Church, constituted of millions of people who are like raindrops through whom the Father is showing forth His glory. To emphasize this need for unity in the Body of Christ, we might learn from the fact that each individual raindrop projects the full spectrum of light, but will only appear as reflecting one color depending upon the observer's point of view. How different each of us appears to one another! And yet, when the whole rainbow is seen by reason of a multitude of drops, the diversity of colors shown is always orderly—in the

same consistent relationship to one another—and is beautiful to behold.

This doctor of science went on to note the precise number of degrees at which light is bent when passing through the raindrop prism producing the rainbow. The mathematical necessities for the position of the sun and raindrops to create the correct prism angle with reference to where we were at two different times of day— *while the rainbow appeared in the same place*—gave us good reason for claiming the appearances at least unbelievable, if not miraculous. There were simply too many variables, and no capacity within us to manipulate them. He argued convincingly that it took more faith to doubt the "rainbow message" to us than to believe it.

In the final analysis, however, we are not basing anything in our past or our future on anything so ephemeral as a rainbow. The roots of our faith are in the Word of God; the Light of our world is the Son of God. That we may be likened to transient raindrops is perfectly acceptable, for ours is only to be, like waters from a fountain, caught up by Himself and poured out where He wills.

In concluding this rainbow experience, I have done as before: shown the consistency with the Word of God and with the testimony of proven, faithful believers. But I have not presented it as a principle. There is obviously no New Testament Principle of Rainbows, so I have not proposed this story to prompt anyone's quest of rainbows.

But I *have* noted these miracles of God's gracious visitations and the unusual timing of natural signs, to underscore one primary fact. He has called His people to worship, and in that atmosphere He will visit them with glory! The glory is His, for He is the source of the light.

But the privilege is ours to receive and disperse that light.

Rainbow Fallout

To this day, what moves me most about that whole episode at the picnic was its signal of God's broad commitment to display His glory ongoingly. Just as He had shown that radiance one day in the sanctuary years before, He now seemed to be indicating a new plateau of His intent to pour forth continued blessing.

God's glory is not a private manifestation for the eyes of the leaders alone, but for His people upon whom He wills to pour that glory like a heavenly radiation fallout;

- A holy fallout infecting each one of us with His righteousness and wholeness; and

- A holy fallout bringing the power inherent in the presence of the King—the power of His Kingdom grace.

Ages ago, Moses said to the Lord, "I beseech thee, show me thy glory." His face would afterward glow with the impress of that encounter.[7] Later, Isaiah prophesied a future day when the glory of the Lord would be upon every home and each assembly place of God's people.[8]

Then Jesus came.

And when Philip said to Him, "Show us the Father and satisfy us," Jesus said, "To look at Me is to see the Father,"[9] which words most poignantly lead us to Paul's glorious statement:

As we, through the mirror of God's revealed truth, look upon the glory of the Lord in the Person of

Jesus, it is thus, with eyes upon Him, that we ourselves are being metamorphosed—that is, progressively and relentlessly changed, transformed into Christ's likeness by the glorious liberating work of the Holy Spirit.

2 Corinthians 3:18 (author's paraphrase)

The flame over each head at Pentecost was in this same genre of God's workings: a distinctly direct and personal manifestation of the same glory. Its presence testifies to the power of the Spirit both to *transform* and *transport;* to *change* each of us into the character of Christ and to *charge* us to touch others with the warmth of His love.

By "rainbow fallout," I mean that God's glory cloud is distilling its radiance wherever people will welcome Him. This glory is for every one of God's people, that all people may see the glory of God in their midst.

The rainbow that evening was God's endorsement of a broadened commitment of one congregation to develop everwidening circles by which His glory might be spread to others. "The glory of the Lord shall be revealed, and all flesh shall see it together."[10] He wants all His people to taste His glory, that they might show it to the nations . . . beginning next door.

And as this glory of God shines through frail, transient humanity, it will become a fulfilled prophecy—a continuum of fulfillment incarnating the Bible's description of the ministering Church; the same words I used as my text that first night at the church so long ago:

But we have this treasure in earthen vessels, that the excellence of the power may be of God and not of us.[11]

Wherever God can find people who will understand and respond to His call, and on His terms, you will find a people who are ever and always "on the way"—in *His* way.

And there will be rainbows.

Notes

[1] Matthew 9:36.

[2] *Rereward* is an older Bible translation's word for an army's rear-guard of defense.

[3] Sheldon Vanauken, *A Severe Mercy* (New York: Harper & Row, 1977), p.189.

[4] 1 Corinthians 11:26.

[5] Ezekiel 1:4–5, 13, 26–28.

[6] Revelation 4:2–3, 6, 8.

[7] Exodus 33:18; 34:29–35.

[8] Isaiah 4:5–6.

[9] John 14:8–9, paraphrase.

[10] Isaiah 40:5.

[11] 2 Corinthians 4:7.